AN ECCENTRIC
GENIUS
MY
NIUS
EXTRAORDINARY
LIFE

JIM EMERTON

Mereo Books

1A The Wool Market Dyer Street Cirencester Gloucestershire GL7 2PR
An imprint of Memoirs Books Ltd. www.mereobooks.com

An Eccentric Genius: 978-1-86151-935-1

First published in Great Britain in 2019
by Mereo Books, an imprint of Memoirs Books Ltd.

The address for Memoirs Books Ltd. can be
found at www.mereobooks.com

Memoirs Books Ltd. Reg. No. 7834348

Typeset in 11/15pt Century Schoolbook
by Wiltshire Associates Ltd.
Printed and bound in Great Britain

CONTENTS

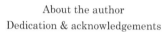

About the author
Dedication & acknowledgements

ABOUT THE AUTHOR

Jim Emerton is a lifelong lover of the countryside and wild creatures whose life has centred on racing pigeons since he was introduced to them by his father at the age of three. He began to rear and race the birds during an idyllic childhood spent mainly in the Lincolnshire Wolds; his mother Dorothy and later his partner Jean worked alongside him in the lofts. The pinnacle of Jim's career came in 1995 when his bird Barcelona Dream set a new British International Championship Club distance record in the renowned Barcelona International race with a record flight home of 879 miles.

When Jim retired from racing in 2006, he donated his 140 birds to the National Flying Club. Since then he has become internationally known as a writer and commentator on the sport and has written a series of books on various aspects of pigeons, the countryside and the wild outdoors.

DEDICATION &
ACKNOWLEDGEMENTS

This book is dedicated to all the people who have enriched my singular life of 70 years duration to date. It has been a life of passion, intensity and fascination.

I would like to give credit to all the teachers, dons, professors, competitors and other characters who have stimulated my myriad of interests in outer and inner worlds, from the tramp to the psychotic to the celebrity. They have made me the personality I am now.

CHAPTER 1

COUNTRY BOY

I was born in the Nightingale Home in Derby on 25th January 1949, the only son of my father Walter James and my mother Dorothy. My parents were living in Derby at the time, but when I was 15 months old we moved to a house at 14 Borough Road, Skegness, overlooking the main road into the town, so my earliest memories are all of Skegness.

I was the last born of the family. My mother had already given birth to three girls, but sadly the first two, born in 1939, were stillborn, an unimaginably dreadful experience after a gruelling 30 hours of labour. They had to wait another seven years before my sister Pat was born in March 1946.

My mother was always a very anxious person. She was again 30 hours in labour giving birth to Pat, and I have always believed it affected her neurologically. She was a restless soul, and maybe that was why we moved so many times. She was very easily upset, and if anything upset her badly she had a habit of flying off to Malta! She loved it there and went, I believe, 22 times. But it gave her energy. She was always a driven sort of person and could never stand to just sit and do nothing – she was like a fly buzzing about.

As the baby of the family and the only boy, I suppose I did receive special treatment. Pat was a very good elder sister and when I was only about 18 months old and she was barely five she would take me for walks. But Pat was too sensitive for her own good, and sadly in later life she attempted suicide by taking an overdose.

Like me Pat loved nature, and as an A-stream grammar school girl she was gifted verbally and given to lovely creative wordplay, puns and jokes. She was a fragile, delicate and somewhat ethereal soul, though she had creative practical skills as well. She was a keen gardener, and she loved to make and sail model boats, which was most unusual for a girl.

My sister inspired me to study and achieve great things. Both she and mother were very bright – in fact we were all creative and sensitive people.

My maternal grandfather Tom was a quiet, kindly man who enjoyed his livestock and gardening, while my grandmother Maud was a matriarchal figure, sharp with money and nobody's fool. My grandfather died at 79, but my grandmother went on until she was 92.

Both my parents were disciplined and conscientious people. My father was philosophical, charming, kind and intelligent, while Mum was very strict and determined, and took a more Victorian attitude to discipline. I often resented her strict regime, as all I wanted to do was wander free in the open air. But she was more artistic and spiritual than my father, and she had a soft side and loved animals.

When I was a boy my father ran a sweet and candy-floss shop in Main Street, Skegness, and for some years he did well by exercising his personal charm and salescraft on his customers. He went into business with his father, my paternal grandfather, running a general store with sweets and tobacco. Everyone liked my father, as he was a clever, kind and charming man. Unfortunately he fell out with my paternal grandad because of a disagreement over how the profits from the business were shared. That created a permanent rift in the family, and we had very little contact with them afterwards. I remember that when my grandfather came to the house once my sister and I both stuck our tongues out at him.

I was a quiet, dreamy, socially inept and deeply sensitive boy, and always avoided the town. I have always hated being hemmed in by town life – I like wide open spaces with nature around me and can't bear to be restricted or kept indoors. The sea was about a mile's walk away from our home in Skegness and further still when the tide was out, but I loved the iodine smell of the ocean, the rides on the donkeys and the visits to Gibraltar Point, the nature reserve which stretches down the coast south of Skegness.

As a young boy, I soon perceived myself to be different. I was a detached, sensitive and dreamy young lad who loved the countryside. Aloof and somewhat claustrophobic, I have never been happy cooped up indoors and I still avoid indoor gatherings wherever possible. All I wanted to do was go off and do my own thing. I started wandering off on my own when I was as young as five years old. I would forget about the rest of the world and escape into my own dream world, losing all sense of time. As a result of this I was always getting into trouble for coming home late and missing mealtimes, and once or twice I got my parents so worried that they called the police. Although I got on well with my sister, she would always back my mother up on occasions like this. I can't really blame her.

I clearly recall my initiation into the wonder and beauty of nature. As a tiny child, not much more than a baby, I was transfixed by some Sweet Williams in the garden, and I have loved flowers ever since. All my life since then l have felt a deep and profound connection with nature, the birds, the elements, the sun, wind and rain, and the wilderness of salt marshes, woods, and all the many wild habitats on the Earth. This love has been matched by an insatiable curiosity, and since the earliest days I have never ceased studying the creatures around me to try to understand them better.

I was drawn to the natural world as soon as I could

walk, and probably earlier. I remember noticing the cotton-wool seed cases of poplar trees shimmering in the gentle warm breeze. My mother would push me in my pram towards the council pond in Skegness, where tiny, magical sticklebacks swam in the clear waters. In 1954, when I was five, Mum took me in short trousers to fish for tiddlers, and I clearly recall my first sight of those little silver fish dangling from the worm.

We lived in Skegness for only a short time before upping sticks again. In 1955, when I was six, we moved to the little village of Skendleby, near Spilsby in the East Lindsey district of the Lincolnshire Wolds, where my parents took on the running of the post office. That was the beginning of perhaps the happiest, most carefree time of my life. We lived in a cottage with three acres of land including an orchard, paddocks and gardens, with an impressive yew tree and a walnut. We had space to keep a variety of pets and livestock. The land was enriched by a population of Chinese pheasants and there was a stray banty hen that produced twelve chicks from the womb of a dry hedge while a young cuckoo called loudly to its parent slave, a little hedge sparrow.

Skendleby was a tiny place with a population of fewer than 200 people and there was wild countryside in all directions. We lived in that village that time forgot for five glorious years, until I was eleven years old. There I was able to live an idyllic, rustic existence. It was in Skendleby that I discovered a love of plants and flowers. I meditated in total abstraction as I watched the spring bulbs, seeing each perfect petal open in my garden of delights. Soon I went out with a spade to a neighbour's wood and dug up snowdrops to add to our collection. It was clandestine and audacious, and very satisfying.

One day I climbed the walnut tree, high into those branches pruned by the winds of time, a symbol of young ambition. I dared to climb to the thin uppermost branches, intoxicated by risk. Finally I descended, racked by anxiety, to the safety of the cushioning grass below. Sadly that tree, a symbol of my worldly and spiritual aspirations, has long gone. We all need trees like that to enrich and grow in the forests of the imagination.

In our three acres of I lived out the boy's adventure

tale, at one with the trees, birds and plants. This dream-like state, occasionally interrupted by adults, would last for five formative years. Part of my soul still haunts that village.

I soon got to know the various wild flowers around Skendleby, as well as butterflies, moths and other insects. I remember being particularly captivated by the ethereal flight of a ghost moth, those strange white skeletal-winged creatures that dance above the grasses on a summer dusk like the ghosts of departed souls.

To be outside in a cool breeze, with ever-changing cloud patterns, was bliss to me as a boy and it remains so now. I can sit with my eyes closed on a spring morning in an oak wood and identify each bird from the orchestra, and the thrilling song of a canary makes my eardrums vibrate. It was the colour, complexity and harmony of the many species that I found fascinating, and I still do. Oh for the glowing euphoria of times past, when a spirit could flow free in the sun, the wind and the rain, and the only roof was the sky!

There were no street lights in Skendleby back in the 1950s and I used to go out and gaze at the stars and watch for meteors. When you take in the wonder of the universe, the egocentric side dissolves and you have a feeling of being at one with the cosmos. I used to have a dimming switch in my bedroom so that the light would gradually fade to darkness, and it became a habit I never grew out of; I still have one now.

My parents tried to drive me to succeed, something which I found hard, as I was always a natural dreamer who preferred to be detached and live in his own world rather than compete with the other lads in the classroom or on the sports field. My mother was a clever woman who won a scholarship to art school, but was never able to take it up because my grandmother wouldn't let her. She was also an accomplished pianist.

I was incredibly shy and did not begin to speak until I was four years old. When I was a little older and gained a little more confidence I began to be something of a thorn in the side to the teachers at my primary school. I was often insolent and received thousands of 'lines' to do as punishment. My teachers never really understood that this was no punishment to me, as I actually liked writing out lines.

It was not until I discovered pigeons that I found

something which truly drove me to seek success and achieve excellence. My father, a calm, kind and gentle man, had introduced me to them when I was three years old. I was instantly hooked by the gentle beauty of the lovely fancy pigeons and cross-bred birds. He kept Tumblers and fancy breeds such as Priests, Nuns, Jacobins and Magpies, although he never raced them because he was simply too kind and gentle to put them through it. As it turned out later, I had no such qualms.

Soon I became aware that there were plenty of stray racing pigeons around (what pigeon men call 'strags' or stragglers, though I didn't know the word then), and with stealth and cunning I used to catch them by luring them with peanuts and then grabbing them, usually with my bare hands. The first stray I saw, at around the age of five, was a young pencil-blue bird, complete with race rubber. It fired my naive wonder and sense of curiosity, and after reporting it we discovered that the little cock belonged to an Irish fancier called Eugene. My old Dad explained to me how pigeon racing worked, and the die was cast.

Although it was through my father that I first discovered pigeons, it was my mother with whom

I mainly shared my love of them as I grew up, and she would become my ally for the rest of her life. I was closer to her than my father, as we shared a love of nature, of natural beauty and the arts, as well as the pigeons which came to dominate my life. I soon became involved in their management. Before long we had bought some brightly-coloured tumblers, and my formative years were spent gazing into the sky at these acrobats of the pigeon world.

Although I always cared far more for the natural world than blackboards and books, I was happy to make an exception for wildlife guides such as the Observers' books. It was not until later that I discovered the wider world of great literature. I didn't have much to say in the classroom at my Church of England primary school, yet I regard this as the happiest time of my life.

Generally I was a strong and healthy lad, though I did have the odd health issue. At the age of five I got appendicitis, I broke a finger at one time playing rugby, and when I was nine I had an accident in the playground which result in breaking my leg in some style, both the tibia and fibula of the lower leg. I spent three months in plaster, and mum used to push me around in a wheelchair. Unfortunately the bone failed to heal straight and they had to rebreak it and reset it – there was no anaesthetic, they just invited me to bite down on something while they snapped it. That did nothing to reinforce my love of humanity.

We had a menagerie of creatures spread over our three acres, and there I was surrounded by, and immersed in, wildlife. Wild geese grazed our paddock, and we bred Dutch, Old English and other breeds of rabbit on our grass paddocks. I spent a lot of time on farms with George and Giles Crust, the sons of a local farmer, who initiated me into field sports of the boyhood kind. Like so many country boys at that time I had a five-shilling Milbro catapult, and I was a mean stone thrower. Later we used .410 shotguns and air rifles and went ratting with terriers, hard-bitten little rascals. We lived wild, climbing trees and collecting birds' eggs in boxes of sawdust, and I loved it all.

We used to scale the inner sanctum of the church belfry in excited admiration of the huge bells, as well as the jackdaws' nests and the nesting feral pigeons. Jackdaws are hardy, clever corvids that may live for 30 years. They form colonies in which there is a clear hierarchical relationship in the pecking order from top to bottom. I admired them for their wily intelligence and survival cunning. The mate of the king jackie becomes the queen, and so on right down to the lowly pariah birds at the bottom of the pile. At Skendleby they used to nest in the chimney pot of our outhouse, and there were dozens nesting in the trees. There were ancient elms in a grove where Giles and George Crust and their sister Lynda and I would examine the eggs by climbing up a web of witches' brooms.

Rabbiting with ferrets was another country pastime I enjoyed at one time. Ferrets can be attractively sleek and furry creatures in the hand, but I always treated them with respect because they will give you a vicious nip, as my friend Brian Plummer's did. It was exciting to stop a warren of rabbits with the purse nets and enter a nice polecat ferret hob (male). The bunnies would spring into the nets, and they do make a lovely casserole of lean high-protein food with country vegetables and gravy. The argument for such pursuits is the control of pests and the balance of nature, yet in truth many do it for sport, and to satiate deeply-held instincts. Men, in particular, may feel compelled to kill, thanks to the ancient and deeply-embedded hunting instinct.

I remember how one day two friends and I netted an old warren at Lower Marishes near Pickering. The warren was so deep that I volunteered to be lowered into it head first as my feet were held. In the dark and feeling forward, I pulled out five live bunnies one by one, and was then pulled out back into the light of day. It was one of those mad, legendary days out in the wilds.

In the winter snows my friend Mick and I went in pursuit of old conies. In the biting wind we heard the distress call of a rabbit, and Mick shot off in his wellies like shit off a stick. Amazingly he came back grasping a live rabbit which had a big old stoat clinging to its neck. Now feral ferrets can be found in the wild, yet I see many a stoat and weasel, and they inhabited my cottage garden. They are truly magical, athletic creatures to behold, especially profiled against the snow.

CHAPTER 2

A FAREWELL TO CHILDHOOD

Life was bliss in Skendleby, but sadly it was not to last. As we entered the 1960s, my parents were finding trade more and more difficult. This was the era of the birth of the supermarket, and little corner shops like ours could not cope with the competition. So new employment was needed, and in 1960 at the age of 11, my primary school years over, we left the village to move back to Derbyshire, to Alvaston on the southern outskirts of Derby. All four of us were extremely upset when we left Skendleby, and I remember my mother crying all the way to Derby in the car.

My parents took over the post office in Babbington Lane before my father was later made chief clerk in Derby, after which my mother continued to run the post office. We lived at 32 Gilbert Street, Alvaston, from 1960, when I was eleven, to 1967, when I left home to go to college. I found moving disruptive and stressful, and this was my fourth home in 11 years. Altogether my parents moved 21 times in their lives, so they never really had time to settle anywhere. I think this affected my mother quite deeply.

However Derby had its benefits, once you got out of the city. My father was a keen angler, and he used to take me to the big lakes at Kedleston Hall on the far side of Derby. The men would use dead bait and live bait for pike while we boys pursued roach, silver bream and other coarse species. We also encountered the primeval lamprey, a fascinating parasitic creature.

As a young angler I enjoyed moderate success in the catching of fish, but of greater significance were the memorable days it brought me in wild and beautiful habitats. Angling requires an intuitive awareness of nature as well as practical skill. We had great fun pulling gudgeon out of a local stream at Alvaston, another chapter in the small boy's dream. I tried for the eels in the dykes of the Wash over many hours, and caught nothing. One day a gang of us grammar school boys descended on Locko Park lake at Spondon, and I remember a day when we pulled out nets of lovely stripy, bristling perch while coots clucked and dragonflies dazzled in the summer air. It was such a perfect day, and all part of boyhood adventure. From minnows to tommy ruffes, stone loach and bullheads, I did enjoy the sport, though I was never to become a dedicated, expert fisherman.

In those years we would take summer holidays in Wales or the Peak District. There was fun when in the summer of 1962, aged 13, I went with my family for a holiday in a chalet in North Wales. In the grounds was a shallow trout stream, where I managed to bag some trout and eels on a night line baited with cockles. Later I would go out with a professional fisherman on the Conway estuary. We baited our lines with soft-back crab (crabs that have just moulted, before their new shells harden) and pulled out juicy dabs and flounders – we even hooked a big turbot. Gently fried in fat, the fish were beautiful to eat.

One day while he was casting into the sea my poor old dad hooked himself in the face, and he was stoical enough not to complain as I teased the big sea hook from his cheek.

My interest in pigeons was stepped up a little when we moved to Alvaston. The city centre had peaceful gardens alongside the river Derwent, and I would travel there on the electric trolleybus and sit catching wily old stray birds with peanuts, put them in a battered fishing creel and take them home. Vagrants snored on the summer lawns, alive with lice and fleas, and one day I got talking to Pigeon Percy, a redoubtable old eccentric. Celebrated in the local paper, he was known as a grand old personality of pigeons. I was highly intrigued by Percy, especially when he would spin his head like a performing Birmingham Roller.

I started getting to know the roller men, the tippler men and the racing men of Derby. Billy Burdett of Alvaston was a feisty, cheerful little character, and he would encourage young me from his wheelchair. He loved his birds and kept several rollers and racers. He did not allow his handicap to inhibit his generosity, for he gave me a big blue racer cock. I would take my birds training in a fishing creel on my motorbike and Billy would say in his broad Derbyshire accent, 'Look at his eye, Jim. Ay'll win Lerwick, ay will'. I took the cock he gave me home and settled it into my loft, pairing it to a chequer pied stray I had caught. After that I was hooked and trained the bird all over, getting around on my motorbike.

In Matthew Street lived Harold Adams, another Roller man, and he gave me his well-known red cock. I enjoyed visiting Harold and lent him the first book I owned about pigeons, *Pigeons And How To Keep Them*. It came back with the pages blackened. He also kept show canaries and helped to initiate me into pigeon racing.

Dr Graham Dexter lived near the Blue Peter in Alvaston. Like me, he kept a kit of Rollers. He was a young man then, before his PhD. Today he is a world authority on competition Rollers and has created the definitive work on them, *Winners With Spinners*. He has judged all over the world and formulated many of the modern rules for competition. Another local pigeon man, Jack Whitehouse, is still a big name today in his 80s.

I spent most of my time during those years at Alvaston either gazing at my roller pigeons or walking the woods and hedgerows. Everywhere we travelled I caught stray racers and brought them home to keep in the loft of the house. Although I was quiet and polite, I was cocky enough to knock on people's doors and charm them into letting me catch roosting strays which I'd spotted on their property. If I spotted a pigeon on someone's window-sill I would say, 'I think that's one of my pigeons up there, do you mind if I come in and catch it?' Yes, I was a cheeky little devil.

So my teenage years, when I wasn't enduring the strict teaching regime at the grammar school, were spent cultivating my Birmingham Roller team or wandering wild in the countryside. I would rush home from school to watch my Rollers perform, a habit which enabled me to develop intense observational skills, although it got a little out of hand because I would never do the homework the academics demanded. As a schoolboy I wrote an essay telling the imaginary tale of clocking a long-distance bird from Marennes, which as things turned out, proved to be prophetic.

My shooting started with a Diana Model 16 which fired tiny darts. By the time I was into my teens I had a Webley Falcon .22 air rifle, a bigger BSA Airsporter .22 air rifle, the most powerful air rifle generally available at that time, and a BSA .410 bolt-action shotgun, and I would often go out in the night with a .410 to stalk rabbits on local allotments at Alvaston. Silence and stealth are your friends in this kind of hunting, as the range of a .410 or an air rifle is very limited. Rabbit stew with dumplings is delicious, but not as delicious as the exhilaration of the chase.

The year we moved to Alvaston I started at Spondon Park Grammar School on the east side of Derby. Among the other new boys was John Shinn, who became a great friend. He had a Meteor air rifle, the BSA equivalent of the Webley Falcon, and we young rascals used our guns to shoot the starlings that feasted on the pears and plums. House sparrows were also legitimate quarry in those days. John was a tough lad who became an engineer, and he developed into an all-round first-class shot.

John and I were notorious for making rude noises in lessons, particularly in English and Geography. This must have annoyed our teacher, Bill Cunningham, because he gave me a lowly grade G for English, even though that was one of my better subjects, and my report read 'Insolent and a thorough nuisance in class, especially in English Literature'. I even got the cane once for lying about my homework. I wasn't so shy at school as I had been back at primary school in Skendleby. My confidence grew as I got older and turned into a big strong lad and a member of the rugby team – I excelled at throwing the cricket ball and even became the arm-wrestling champion. I was certainly never bullied.

John was good at English Grammar and I gained inspiration from sitting next to him. In fact, despite my behaviour, I got on well with my English teacher and did eventually get a good grade at O-Level. John was a big, strong, rugged fellow and his dad Maurice, who was a policeman, supplied me with a twelve-bore shotgun and a Remington .22 bolt-action hunting rifle. We grew up together playing for the school rugby team and did a lot of rough shooting, which I loved.

The main gun I used for rough shooting and

wildfowling was a cheap Spanish Ligano Herald Mark 2 twelve bore. It was heavily choked for range and accounted for everything from snipe to wild geese.

John's father's job didn't seem to stop him from being an inveterate poacher who roamed the Derbyshire countryside. One Sunday morning he took us stealthily out in his 1930s Rover to try to shoot the grouse that would sit on top of the walls that crossed the moors. I spotted an old hare, its ears poking up just above the wheat, and in a haze of excitement I shouted 'stop the car!' and shot it with my .22 rifle. I also remember John jumping over a hedge to retrieve two English partridges we had shot in front of some farm cottages. John was an eccentric, but he became a great wildfowler and later hunted African game.

One morning, in pursuit of shooting rights for rough shooting, I jumped on my Claude Butler racing bike and headed off down Shardlow Road, calling at every farm on the way to ask for permission. It was another exercise in my usual persistence, and it took me as far as a village called Wilson in Leicestershire. Here a kindly farmer gave me express permission to shoot over 300 acres of fields, hedgerows, railway line and copse. I was in rough shooting heaven, and after that I walked the land regularly with my side-by-side 12 bore with full and half-choke barrels. Coveys of English partridges paused to grit on the disused railway line, which made good habitat for them as they like dry terrain. They were excellent shooting and good eating, along with the wily old cock pheasants, rabbits, hares and the odd duck. In those days I went with a .22 rifle slung over my shoulder for attempts at sniping long-range quarry – rather macho at the time.

I would often get up and go out at the crack of dawn with my Labrador Ben, my first dog, acquired in 1965 when I was 16, and walk the stubble fields, the woods and hedges to flush out pheasants, partridges, rabbits and hares and flight the woodpigeons coming into roost. I was developing the skill you need to become a good shot.

Dogs have been my companions through many of my own adventures in the wild. Ben was a lovely, brave old dog. As a puppy he spent the first night in bed with me to 'socialise' him. His initial training was done by a keeper who knew his dogs. With my Acme call whistles and staghorn stop whistle I would learn to control him, and he became a loyal and obedient and special friend. Ben happily swam dykes, climbed bushes and jumped barbed wire fences to retrieve rabbits and assorted game. I bowled over an old hare from the safety of the sea wall one early, misty Sunday morning, and the old boy jumped a fence, swam the dyke and brought the animal to hand.

I well remember the day a single woodie appeared at long range and I took it, a very sporting shot. 'Hi lost!' I called, and the dog raced off to retrieve the single pigeon. Ages came and went by with no sight of Ben. When I went to investigate, I found him straddling dense bramble bushes and attempting to climb up to the fork of a hawthorn tree.

In later years Dad took Ben to the office each day. What a lovely game dog he was. It was a sad day in 1980 when I buried him under the old apple trees at Sycamore Cottage, Holtby, where we lived from 1978.

After that I was keen to find a replacement, but it was five years before I found the right one. Freddie the Jack Russell was born in 1985 on a farm at Lower Marishes in Yorkshire and belonged to my wife Jean's mother. He was a canny dog and could interpret in his canine way what I was thinking. He was an expert footballer, and his claim to fame was climbing up to the cottage roof on the clematis. When I pulled him down, there was a fat rat in his mouth. I loved that dog, and even now as I write more than 30 years on a tear forms in my eye.

Jumping forward a few years for a moment, when Freddie died many years later, Jean's mum was bereft and complained that she was lonely. I knew a coursing greyhound man from Rufforth called Ray Wilson, who said he had a nice little retired bitch of Irish origin calld Lady Jane Cooneen. With great anticipation, Jean and I went to collect her. A huge, athletic dog bounded up the paddock to greet us and Ray introduced us to this beautiful tiger-striped bitch. Off we shot in the Clio van to show Jean's mum, who was shocked by her size, but delighted, and we left the old lady open-mouthed with her new love. Lady Jane had bad teeth and as a result her breath really ponged, but Jean's mum didn't mind.

We had a hilarious experience once when the poor old lady panicked because the dog had apparently vanished, only to be found stuck fast behind the settee. A lovely quiet animal was that old dog. She would take a rabbit on the lead with one snap of her jaws as we were walking along Holtby lane. She won more than 12 firsts and became the spiritual companion of my mother until she was 92. Jean's mother's dying words to me were 'Look after Jane'. Sadly every dog goes the way of all flesh in the end, but Jane lived on until she was 13 years old.

I was never a hunting man, but I would watch the fox hunts around Holtby. The hunt is primal and instinctual and understandably it may be perceived as cruel by thoughtful and compassionate people, as may any pursuit where sentient lifeforms are exploited for human gratification. Sometimes the hounds would come into my garden. Working beagles are nice dogs to see, but the hunting of brown hares is banned, as they are in decline due to intensive farming, poaching, hunting and loss of optimal habitat. Before it was banned I used to go along with the Old Yorkshire Coursing Club. There were some clever dogs to see in full gallop, yet many of the fit, fly and strong hares escaped.

I have seen Blue Hares, or Mountain Hares, as well as the Brown Hare of the southern lowlands. They are wonderful, athletic animals. In my cruel and rural youth I walked the fields of Derbyshire and Leicestershire with a 12-bore in hand to bag hares for the pot, which I would put in the poacher's pocket of my Barbour Solway Zipper. I wore it to shreds within six months, going through hedges and barbed wire fences. It was a delight to see Ben retrieve them to hand, big as they are, being up to 9 lbs in weight. He was a lovely old boy and a grand working dog. They are excellent eating. Sadly the Brown Hare is declining as a result of the profit agenda of intensive agriculture and the associated degradation of habitat.

Hunting with dogs is a traditional sport in the UK, as it is in most countries of the world, although hunts are of course no longer allowed to kill foxes deliberately either. Ratting with hardnosed terriers is a different matter entirely. It is both lethal and exciting – the dogs go into a frenzy and the rats squeak in terror. Many of the old traditions continue under cover, although banned by law.

The wildest dogs I have seen are African hunting dogs, which have a very strong pack instinct. All our dogs are descendants of Lupus the wolf, and the timber wolf in full cry under the moonlight is my favourite animal. It is the epitome of nature, the very call of the wild, for the wolf is a rugged, instinctual and highly intelligent creature.

It may seem a paradox that a young man who loves nature should want to take the lives of beautiful birds and animals, but it is based on deep-rooted instincts born of ancient man's need to survival, the instinct to claim wild creatures for the pot. As a country boy I was driven from the beginning by the deeply instinctual, primal urge of the hunter. I was in my element out in the wind, rain and snow and sometimes under the moon at night. The thrill of the chase was both intoxicating and electrifying.

CHAPTER 3

THE WILD GOOSE MAN

In 1965, when I was 16 years old, my shooting career took a dramatic turn, thanks to the start of a friendship with one of the great men of the sport, Kenzie Thorpe. 'The Wild Goose Man', as he was known, also the title of his best-selling biography by Colin Willock, was not a just a skilled wildfowler and general shot but a noted poacher, ex-jailbird, middleweight boxing champ and all-round eccentric. He was also a talented artist who worked with Sir Peter Scott.

It started when my friend John Shinn responded to an advertisement in *Shooting Times & Country Magazine*, the shooting man's weekly. Kenzie was inviting people to stay on his houseboat and study the birds, seals and other wildlife of the Wash, that wild, rugged and remote wilderness of tidal creeks, sea lavender and samphire which lies on the east coast not much more than 70 miles from Derby, and I was eager to join my friend on this great new adventure. We were driven down in an Austin Cambridge and out into the wilderness at the famous Shep White's, beyond the flat potato fields, with quaint village characters and an abundance of brown hares and pheasants. It was raining heavily, so during final trek across open creeks and saltings to Kenzie's houseboat we managed to scatter our provisions all over the marsh.

At dawn the great man, Mackenzie Thorpe himself, arrived to meet us. His eyes were deep with knowledge, his face craggy with wind and salt exposure, and he cut a unique and solitary figure in that bleak landscape. He greeted us by snapping that we were late – he was a tough master. This was the start of two young boys' greatest adventure game, as we roughed it out to the stalk edges, the sandbanks and the edge of the North Sea with the greatest wild goose man of all time. He called John 'Hawkeye', while I was 'the Boy'.

John and I embraced nature full on as we learned the Wash's secrets; the hordes of waders, the ducks and geese, the marsh harriers floating by on the wind and the wily marshland pheasants as they tried to evade the gun. We lived the boy's adventure tale, and those times by the sea would colour my life forever. The saltings were a wild, rugged and remote wilderness of tidal creeks, sea lavender and samphire. We gathered potatoes from the local fields and cooked them on a paraffin stove in sea water scooped from the ocean.

At high spring tide the boat lifted on its moorings and you found yourself floating at the edge of the North Sea. A cloud of fog enveloped the boat and the calls of the common seals were intensified by the murky dampness. At times like this my imagination was fired and my fears of the wild intensified – would the moorings break and the boat float out into the eternal sea?

The sound of wild geese in the estuary is primal and elemental, and thrills you to the bone. First you hear faint sounds from afar and then there comes a clamour overhead and in a moment they become your world. On the Wash the winds blow in from Siberia, and at times they will lift you off the sea wall. You come alive in remote wilderness and on the edge of survival. You know you are one small soul in the great web of vibrant life on earth, and far from the madding crowd of city torment. It is a place where men may become giants of the spirit, alone in the vastness of life.

It turned out that Kenzie had quite a history. He was one of eight children born to a Romany father in the early years of the century. Married with children himself and struggling to make ends meet in the post-war years, he took up poaching, mainly hares, pheasants and partridges, and sold them to local butchers. He preferred to do his poaching in bad weather, because he knew it was unlikely that anyone else would be around to see him, and it is easier to approach wild creatures when your movements are masked by wind and rain. The early hours of Monday morning were a good time, because Kenzie reasoned that the keepers would have been drinking all weekend and would still be sleeping it off. His record was 93 pheasants off one man's land. He would get caught on occasion, usually when he was coming home in the early morning.

He had built the houseboat from cedarwood with the help of a group of friends; it was his second home as he also had a conventional house in Sutton Bridge. He had met Peter Scott out shooting (actually poaching, in Kenzie's case) in 1928 and became his assistant when Scott built a wildfowl centre on the marsh. During the war he joined a gang building pill-boxes along the sea wall and briefly served in the Navy (he was discharged as medically unfit). He finally gave up poaching in the 1950s to devote his time to wildfowling and guiding.

In January 1970 I spent my 21st birthday by myself on Kenzie's houseboat, and met up with a fowler and his son from Rotherham. Geese were flighting in and out of the potato fields while I listened with eager ears from the gangplank. There was intense anticipation as I sneaked into a tidal creek by the sluice beyond Shep White's. It was a flight in the twilight, and three geese came in range. Sweeping the gun skyward, I dropped one out onto the sea lavender. Old Kenzie said 'Trust you to bag a rarity', for the bird was a yellow-billed bean goose (now a protected species). They may be found in the company of the more common pinkfoot. The party ended in singular satisfaction.

In the Wash estuary the marshland birds were difficult quarry, calling for acute senses and sharp shooting. Imagine being alone in murky rain by twilight attempting to bag diminutive jack snipe and golden plover (both protected now) with a 12-bore. You need to be very spry to bring home even one of these fast and canny waders. A right and a left is some result when the odds of cold gloom are stacked against you. You will pit all your resolve and exploit all your senses in pursuit of these lovely migrants from Spitzbergen and Greenland. It is most exciting to roast the kill afterwards, as it reflects ancient ritual.

Alone in wilderness and down to your instincts, you may learn some serious lessons in life. Stripped of the veneer of society, you gain a sense of stark reality. A walk along the sea wall under the moon and stars is both eerie and enchanting. The corollary is that a true wilderness man can never be happy back in the life of the city.

Many of my sweetest moments have been within the sight and sound of wild birds. I recall a flight of whooper swans, highlighted by sun on grey cloud, filling my hungry eyes with beauty. Later I asked Kenzie to depict the scene in oils on canvas. It was real experience I sought, not passively taking in imagery from the TV.

Wild geese and the challenge of shooting them in near-darkness are embedded in wildfowling folklore. Many rough shooting men will never manage to bag an estuarine pink. The Wash wilderness selects out the case-hardened individuals who will sit out in a frozen tidal creek in a gale of lashing snow. I still shiver at the memory of an all-night vigil in January with Dave Twedell from ABC College in 1968, when we were young, daft and free. The total bag was two frozen sets of bones.

One night I was out on a wild and lonely evening flight on the Wash marshes, with the sea foaming in on a high spring tide. The scudding clouds in a refreshing gale sharpened my senses, and I heard and spotted brent geese, common scoters (not so common now) and the beautiful shelduck. My brain was buzzing with anticipation: this was an experience that only wilderness can create.

Then, as I lay in hiding among the boulders, a great flight of teal emerged from the flashes to the right. I pulled out three together with the right barrel and one with the left as they sprang skyward. I cooked and ate all the birds after this intoxicating experience in the remote elements, although the execution of it was clinical. In the wilderness you touch base and find your soul and spirit.

Back to the marsh. I had forgotten the torch, a silly slip as the saltings are harsh and unforgiving. Kenzie had issued the order 'Three-thirty by the little bush', and I realised it would be a daunting prospect to find a small bush in the dark. I opened the houseboat door and stepped off the gangplank into the marsh and the chill night air. It was like walking into a black hole, but the tingle of the marsh wind on my face and the whiff of iodine were intoxicating.

My progress along the sea wall was tortuous, and fear only compounded its difficulty. The creeks leading to the safety of the wall were tougher than an SAS assault course. I knew it was best to probe and feel with the toes through your thigh waders while gauging the width and depth of the tidal creeks. I also knew I had to protect my gun at all costs, as salt water is death to steel barrels and actions. However the difficulty of my passage only heightened perception and increased my desire to meet my guide and mentor by the little bush as arranged. I arrived safely at the sea wall, panting but relieved and proud. How commanding was the darkness and the lunar remoteness of the Wash saltings.

I carried on at a comfortable pace, each step taking me gradually closer to my destination. The red light of the observation tower caught my attention. Then, further along the sea wall, I came to a farmhouse. My eyes and ears were alert for every changing facet of the night scene. The stout supports of the 'dark tower' lingered on; there were all too few landmarks in this endless horizon. A whistling wind made sounds more audible, like the startled roosting pigeon, quick to leave the safety of its perch and disappear like a passing cloud into the night sky. The few trees, mainly sycamore, were massive, their branches long forced to point inland by the marsh wind sweeping its way down from the Arctic.

The house appeared dark and threatening in my young mind and I imagined it to be some medieval relic, the haunt of an ancient demon. I did not dare to tread down in the shadows where the sea wall dropped down to it. I glanced warily behind to make sure I was alone.

In the distance I spotted a faint light moving rhythmically. It was Kenzie, and I had found the bush, a shrubby little hawthorn and our signpost to the way to deep and fruitful creeks.

Kenzie muttered a gruff 'Morning'. I was not pleased to see that with him were two more wildfowlers, smartly-dressed middle-class types. 'We've just come from the bridge at a hundred miles an hour in an E-type,' Kenzie told me, not sounding too impressed. The men looked like townie jet-setters to me, overdressed in tweeds and over-equipped.

I was excited, yet I remained self-possessed as we struck off over the marsh. We followed the line of some good flat marsh used for grazing along the false bank and took our stations along a nice shell-bottomed creek. I settled into a comfortable position to await the expected, or the unexpected. A Second World War walkie-talkie carrier proved ideal for use both as a pillow and a haversack. You could shoot seated, kneeling or lying back for the most difficult shots. In the vast open spaces of the saltings visibility is crucial, while not to be seen yourself is imperative. In those days the quarry could be godwit, curlew, golden plover or grey plover as well as ducks and geese.

Dawn that morning would come at about 6 am. It would be a long wait, so a clear mind was essential. The cold and discomfort heightened our alertness and helped us to resist drowsiness and torpor.

The spring tide started to creep its way through the myriad creeks, and soon swirls of water were appearing. Waders in their thousands could be heard bubbling away in their gregarious and often hysterical fashion. The sharp, eerie cries of curlew were audible; they would soon flight to higher marshes and their dawn feeding on the great grasslands.

Several godwit – legal quarry back then – flew by in the half-light, but they were out of range. I heard no shots. Perhaps this would be a blank night.

Then I heard the clear trill of a curlew. I shrank back into cover in case the bird came within range of the full-choke barrel. I heard Kenzie call to the bird, which momentarily veered into the wind in response and promptly fell to his shot.

No more shots were fired that morning. Back at the sea wall, Kenzie remarked laconically, 'We've done well, one call, one shot, one bird, and that's how it should be done'. It was a lesson to the E-Type pair, who had no doubt expected a mass slaughter of the wildfowl population of the marshes. We separated and Kenzie began the walk back, to return later with more eager clients, while I began the long trek back to his houseboat.

Fourteen days on Kenzie's houseboat on the Wash saltings would heighten your senses and stimulate your imagination. Sometimes mice crawled along the bilges and ventured out at night on food sorties. Kenzie issued a challenge about one particular mouse – 'Bet you can't get 'im'. From then on, to conquer that little animal became an *idée fixe*, even an obsession.

That night, before bunk time, I set the trap. It must not fail! Cheese tends to crumble into flakes, affording a safe meal for the raider, so I daubed the spike with butter. Then I extinguished the Tilley lamp and waited, hardly daring to breathe or blink in the near blackness. The vast loneliness and emptiness of the marshes outside seemed to penetrate the woodwork of the boat.

The silence was broken by an erratic scraping; my mouse had come to explore. I heard chewing and scratching as our little invader raided the sugar bag, a damp and dirty store of near-solid sugar. Suddenly the scrapings stopped, to be followed by a loud twang – the trap had sprung! I flicked on the torch and collected my prize with great satisfaction. Such simple pleasures remain strong in the minds of men.

Rodents are fascinating animals, and none more so than the brown rat, despicable creature as it is and credited with every possible evil and malevolent power. The rat is seen as the epitome of filth and despised by humans the world over. However there are those who credit it with the praiseworthy qualities of intelligence and cleanliness.

As I was sitting one night in my bunk on the houseboat after struggling to get to sleep, a shaft of moonlight came through the wired-up window. Just then I heard a piercing squeal – a rat. I decided to attack. I stealthily slid from my bunk and reached for the goose gun, feeling the cold metal in the dark. I slipped two BB cartridges into the chambers and slunk like a cat towards the door. I opened it to see several rats playing around the gangplank.

I took careful aim and fired – and missed. I had forgotten that at such close range with choke barrels the shot pattern, though lethal, would be far too narrow for an easy kill.

The Wash wildfowler must treat discipline as his watchword. The marsh can be unpredictable, and it can quickly claim the life of the innocent or unwary. Man is the interloper here, and this flat wilderness can do fine without us. It is all too easy, through over-excitement, fear or stupidity, to fall foul of this inhospitable place. As a young man I was foolhardy and unyielding, even when the bounds of caution had been reached.

I was out on the marsh in the dark of an early morning with a slight fog. This was not going to stop me as I had planned a morning flight, hopefully at the geese. I trekked out to the stalk edges and found a nice creek, good and deep but narrow enough for concealment. The atmosphere was still and heavy with damp, and the darkness was impenetrable. This was a lonely place, and now eerie wisps of thicker fog were now starting to form. These soon joined up to form banks of fog which were so dense that I knew all chances of a goose had gone. I also knew that I would now have to return to the safety of the houseboat before the conditions deteriorated any further.

I looked around for a marker or reference point, but nothing was visible. Fear began to creep upon me, and despite the cold I was beginning to feel hot under my Solway zipper and with all my gear. At first I staggered around in all directions trying to find a recognisable creek or channel, but it was impossible to see anything. I had made the mistake of not bringing a compass, because I had always felt they were for nancies.

Suddenly a familiar noise pierced the fog – the sound of a car passing on the other side of the sea wall. Thank god for that, I grunted to myself. Now I knew which way I had to go. I plunged off into the void, panting and with heart thumping. But something was wrong. As I floundered across the marsh the mud seemed to get softer and deeper, and worse, the tide was now rising and filling the creeks around me, and I could smell kelp. Then I heard the sound again from in front of me – but this time I realised that it was not a car at all. It was the foghorn of a ship out on the North Sea. I was going the wrong way and charging towards danger.

I turned around and floundered back away from the sound, to reach the safety of the sea wall at last. I was safe, but how easily I could have drowned a lonely death that morning out on the marsh, trapped by mud and a rushing tide.

Danger is endemic in many field sports, and many people lose their lives in the wild places of the world to the gun, the mountain, the sea and other natural hazards. In 1967 Kenzie and I encountered an uncharted danger zone in the tidal creeks of the Wash marshes. With a cat tide rising at a great rate, we were cut off by the fast-flowing muddy depths of a large artery. The old rogue saved my life that day, by feeling for a raised sandbank with his thigh wader, and that was good enough for me to risk following him to safety.

On another morning, in 1967, Kenzie and I surveyed the high spring tide as it flooded in towards the sea wall at Shep White's on the Wash saltings. Old Kenzie proclaimed that there was only one man in Lincolnshire who could reach the houseboat on foot in a rising cat tide. Now there's a challenge, I thought to myself. With fear and trepidation I followed the great man out, echoing his every crafty move as survival mode kicked in. After some anxiety and sweat we both reached the moored boat, and soon we were afloat on the inexorable tide.

Kenzie did not restrict his shooting to the Wash and its wildfowl – he was a great pigeon shot too. The humble woodpigeon is found everywhere, and is getting still more numerous – there are more than half a million of them in Britain now. The woody has great qualities as a sporting bird as well as on the table. It has beauty, cunning and a devastating turn of speed when it needs it, and it is second only to the curlew in the variety of shots it offers. The curlew of course is now protected, but the pigeon can be shot all the year round. It is unfortunate that the powers that be have recently changed the law on shooting woodpigeons so that you are now allowed to kill them only to protect crops, not for sport or to eat them, despite the fact that these birds are so numerous, so they certainly do not need protection, and of course they are a cheap and tasty source of wild food.

Inland, Lincolnshire and Cambridgeshire offer some of the best pigeon shooting in the country, so my old pal Shinny and I arranged to tackle them with Kenzie during our summer holidays. Naturally we made the houseboat our HQ, as it was isolated and cheap and could be made comfortable. We looked forward eagerly to our forays with the master. I say 'master' because even in his sixties, Kenzie could wipe pigeon out of the sky as neatly as if he was wiping away with a feather duster. Any pigeon that was unfortunate enough to fly within range was usually a dead one.

Our transport was a 1930s Fiat which was little more than a two-seater glass bubble, but even so it was an improvement on the previous Ford Popular. We collected Kenzie from his home in Sutton Bridge, a journey of some 12 miles along tortuous lanes and dykes from Shep White's. We loaded up the diminutive car with the pigeon gear, I squeezed into the back and we set off on the long drive to Cambridgeshire. Thornley was the destination, a name which has become well known for its pigeon shooting. On arrival we took a long track which bordered huge fields before stopping and walking along a railway line which flanked a series of dense woods which were obviously the main roosting area. Pigeons were clattering out of every available niche and roosting in the trees or even on the ground.

John trekked off into the distance to try to find a spinney, while Kenzie put me in the thick of the wood. I was feeling a sense of occasion as I bent the natural cover over, ten-foot-high burdocks bearing fruit, to provide concealment, which was soon virtually total.

I crouched down like a dog fox and waited for the birds to flight. They soon came thick and fast, and I was shooting constantly. That day it seemed I could do nothing wrong; confidence is a great thing in shooting, and mine was riding high that day. The first bird arrived at 3 pm, and the shooting continued for a further one and a half hours. I was connecting with everything I fired at. Two birds approached side by side, and both fell to my shots. A single bird approached at great speed at the limit of range; I raised the gun and it fell lifeless to earth.

Unknown to me, Kenzie was watching his young protégé. 'Hell of a shot!' he cried. He came over to collect my bag. 'There must be fifty-five birds out there,' he declared. Intensely proud, I walked back the 50 yards or so to the railway line. Even here, the track was littered with pigeons. 'You're the best young shot on pigeons I've ever had out with me,' he said.

I tried to contain my newly-inflated ego as Shinny lumbered up self-consciously from the spinney with a mere three pigeons. He had not shot so well that day.

I was soon brought back down to Planet Earth when I missed a simple shot on the way back to the car. A further hide some yards away brought equal rewards, and pigeons and stock doves were falling to the gun. It was a memorable experience.

Kenzie and I had another successful assault on the pigeons when we set off one day to Holbeach St Marks. The site was a bean field, this crop being greatly loved by pigeons, and we had collected a couple of characters from Buxton Gun Club. I had my reservations about their excited boasts about their prowess. I feel a hunter should be like a silent assassin and should preferably operate alone, although I accept that many see a shoot as a social occasion with friends gathered to shoot together. But I believe the essence of shooting is the lone individual relying on his wits who strikes as efficiently as any natural predator to make his mark on nature.

Once again Kenzie put 'the Boy' in a favourable position, while the other two guns were relegated to the lean side of the field. Pigeons floated past in droves and I was soon shooting strongly. The sky was turning steely grey, with the pigeons whirring past a darker grey against it.

Kenzie was watching again. 'You're shooting well but wild,' he said. Immediately I started to tone down my approach and shoot with more control and deliberation. Good pigeon shooting is about quietly despatching the birds from the air into a well-defined killing zone. There will be an optimum distance at which the experienced gun can kill quickly and efficiently.

We saw the afternoon out kneeling in the mud. The bag was fairly modest, about 50 pigeons in all, of which the two 'experts' accounted for about seven. Kenzie was complaining of a painful knee, and it was this injury which years later finally forced him to give up his wildfowling adventures.

Old Kenzie took many well-known people shooting, and I remember him taking the actor James Robertson

Justice punt gunning. He was once visited by Prince Charles, who told him he was aware that Kenzie had been poaching on the Sandringham Estate! Presumably HRH was not there for recrimination. Kenzie passed away in 1976 at the age of 68, after which, by Romany tradition, the houseboat was torched.

The old boy remains a great character in my nostalgic imagery. The Wash was the habitat of many eccentric hard cases, and I loved them all.

Careless use of guns inevitably costs lives in the field from time to time, as the effect of an ounce or more of shot is horrific at close range, hence the need for great attention to safety. When I was shooting with Kenzie and others our gun safety code was meticulous and over very many years we shot without incident and lived to tell the tale and with all our limbs intact. If you live to a good age, you are enjoying the benefits of shrewd and wise decisions, unless of course you have simply had a charmed life.

Fishing too can be dangerous in rivers, lakes and oceans. Alone on the boat on one occasion, a gale and a spring tide threatened to float me out into the Wash at night with moorings broken. That fired my imagination, as I could have been doomed. You must respect nature, as it will often try to claim your life.

There are other fates awaiting the hunter besides drowning. More than one fisherman has been taken by a crocodile, and in 1984 the wife of a Danish angler who was fly fishing for trout in the Aberdare Mountains of Kenya was killed by a lion.

Over the years my spiritual love for the natural world overcame the ruthless killing spirit, which was overwhelmed by love, compassion and reverence for nature's wonder and beauty. These days I feel a fine poem is a far greater achievement than a dead bird. I shot my last old cock pheasant in 1980 in the apple orchard at Sycamore Cottage, Holtby, York. I stalked it and despatched it with my BSA Airsporter air rifle, and the bird was an old one, as tough as teak to eat. I eventually gave the 12-bore and the Airsporter to John, and the Remington was surrendered to the police.

An encounter with a red fox was instrumental in persuading me to hang up my gun. In a field hedgerow in Chellaston, Derbyshire, we looked each other in the eye and I knew that I must not shoot. I realised in that intense moment that we were all united in nature, all joint life forms on Planet Earth. The fox in its dance is a mesmerising sight, so graceful and beautiful. The prey may be a grasshopper, a vole or a rabbit. Foxes, led by hungry vixens, forage on carcasses in my garden, and I have been observing them since I was a young boy. Every facet of cunning and near-human intelligence is demonstrated by old Reynard. I love the way they lope along so confidently in close proximity to humans.

I do feel that man can be perceived as cruel in manipulating, exploiting and preying on birds and animals. Although, like many men as they grow older, I no longer, hunt, fish or shoot, I recognise that some men will always feel the urge to hunt as a primal and instinctual response to a natural urge bred in us in the days when we were primitive creatures who relied on our hunting skills for the survival of ourselves and our families. These days many hunt with binoculars, camera or paintbrush, which can produce exactly the same thrill and sense of being at one with nature.

CHAPTER 4

AN INTELLECTUAL EMERGES

Despite all the horseplay and the running wild, I must have learned something in the classroom during my grammar school years, because I managed to leave Spondon at 16 with four O-levels. I have my late sister Pat to thanks for firing my inner imagination with the proclamation that she had six O-levels to my mere four, which woke me up to desire and to ambition just in time and coloured my life ever after. I also owe a debt of gratitude to the educational system for my years at grammar school and the eleven years that followed on college courses. They taught me mental discipline and control, particularly under the pressure of an examination.

There was nothing very intellectual about the job I did when I left school in 1965, aged 16, because I went to work as a garden boy at Darley Abbey Park. That opportunity came out of attending a careers convention at school, where they recommended an apprenticeship with Derby Parks Department, and as a grammar school boy I was fast tracked. I got paid £3 for a 44-hour week – one shilling and fourpence an hour, or about seven pence in today's money. Backs were bent and discipline was strict, and the head gardener, John Graham, who was always smartly dressed in a bowler hat, was God. He once appeared on *This Is Your Life*. Parks gardening in those days was a world of craftsmen, and many earthy characters, from labourers to the esteemed propagator, exchanged colourful and amusing stories in their insular and specialist world.

It was pure bliss for a bright young apprentice to be surrounded by all those exotic herbaceous plants, endless borders humming with bees and wafting summer butterflies. Dull winter days found us washing clay pots with scrubbing brushes in a brass well of cold water. A more skilled task was the crocking of endless plant pots, to be lined with roughage. Those were the days when skill and craft were precious and learned through toil and study.

Since I excelled in my chosen horticulture, in 1967 at the age of 18, still introverted and naïve, I was sent to Askham Bryan College in York for two years of advanced study in Recreational and Decorative Horticulture, a move which forced me to part with some newly-acquired racing pigeons. Although I had to lose those birds, I never stopped catching strags.

There followed a period of solid study and self-indulgence. By now I had begun to discover the hidden intellectual within, something which none of my friends or family had any reason to suspect existed during my adolescent years at Spondon Grammar. At the age of fifteen or sixteen I became fixated on botanical Latin, learning the names of all the plants I encountered. Systematic learning was now the great attraction.

At Askham Bryan, I found myself truly intoxicated by horticulture. I passed most of my times as an aloof and detached bookworm, but my studies were punctuated by some much less cerebral incidents. Walking out one day through the local woods I came upon a baby crow, and decided that it should live in a box on the window sill of my cloister. Soon after this the cleaning lady was clearing out the fluff from under the bed when the bird uttered an almighty caw from the depths of its box. She let out a shriek of shock, and I had to face the music with the Vice Principal, who asserted that keeping a live crow in my room was taking a love of nature a little too far. The crow had to go, but I could not be without a bird in my care, so that night I went out into the grounds and plucked a young woodpigeon from a hawthorn tree.

Sports day between us 'hortics' was an epic battle with the predominant 'agrics'. We won in pathetic style the slow bicycle race and the cricket ball throwing contests, in which I broke the college record, winning a tiny cup for my achievement. At that time I still remained unbeaten at arm wrestling.

Wednesday afternoons were notable for our indulgence in rough shooting on the estate, and I kept my 12-bore and a bandolier of cartridges in the wardrobe of my room (this was 1968, when it was still possible to do such a thing). I loved this primal and focused activity, an elemental and instinctual outlet for a young tyke's inner nature. The dressing of a brace of hares in my room was perhaps taking primalism a little too far. The meals served on wooden benches by adorable and homely cooks were delicious, and the spectacle of a suckling pig ceremony was institutional, historic and awesome. Our every whim was satisfied – coffee made with milk, a snooker room, a juke box and every conceivable delight.

I spent the summer of '68 toiling in all weathers on York parks for little pay, polite, naive and bright-eyed. Soon I encountered a foreman, a kind and good-natured man called Peter Cook. To give me a break from the mindless and back-breaking work, he took me home for tea and showed me his much-loved cacti and tomato plants. Convinced by then that grown-up life was all conscientious hard grind, I recall Mr Cook man with affection. Oh, that all the middle management would prove to be his equal.

Working on the expansive open space of Rowntree Park, there were some colourful and memorable events. On and off, I put in the years with sweat, blood and tears, until there came a pivotal and life-changing day in February 1969 when I attempted to tow Bob, the man in charge, behind my Mini-van to bump-start the antiquated bonza truck. I managed to rip part of the back of the van off. Bob, to his credit, was an honest man, although touched by some nervous quirks.

With Bob I hatched a cunning plan to cull the resident flock of fantail pigeons down to the brightest and healthiest specimens. This murderous spree was rumbled by the resident park keeper, and it created a furore, extending to the chief executive of the council. To this day, I respect the fact that poor old Bob took it all on the chin.

A jovial character called Charlie also worked in the park. When he made an ambitious attempt to light a stove, traces of fuel found their way onto his hair and caught fire. I extinguished them with raw speed.

At the end of the two years I graduated from Askham Bryan with distinction in City & Guilds Stage II in Horticulture. My teachers at Spondon would have been amazed to learn that I had secured a place at no less than the hallowed and exotic Royal Botanic Gardens in Kew.

October 6 1969 marked the start of a dramatic period of my life. I was admitted to the Royal Botanic Gardens at Kew, described as an internationally important botanical research and education institution, to study for a Diploma in Horticulture and qualify as a teacher of rural studies. My beloved Roller pigeons, my shooting interests and the gentle times in wild countryside had to be left behind for the next three years as I submitted to the much more constrained life of an institutionalised student.

In the event I loved the intense academic life at Kew, which taught me intellectual rigour and mental discipline in the pursuit of truth and the realisation of objectives. The pursuit of perfection in my subjects brought me five honours in the first year and made me top student.

There were some gifted people at Kew, and one of them was a certain Alan Titchmarsh. Alan was a sanguine and affable fellow whose easy manner belied his determination to get to the top. On the day we started, Alan and I were among those who posed for the course photograph, and my first digs was a room with him at No. 83 Mortlake Road, Kew, described in his 2003 book *Trowel and Error*:

I beheld an elderly lady in an old-fashioned pinny with grey hair and classes over which she peered at me... I stepped over the threshold into a dark hallway, decorated with even darker Victorian wallpaper... she pushed open the door of what amounted to a cupboard, with a small window and a smaller wardrobe. It had two sources of illumination: a 25-watt bulb suspended directly from the ceiling and the mercury vapour street lamp directly outside... And then there was the bed. The first time I turned it down I noticed some small creatures on the sheet... they disappeared quite quickly. I woke up the following morning with an impressive selection of pink spots which itched like mad.

Alan and I shared a dingy attic room with a bare flex hanging from the ceiling with just that 25-watt light bulb hanging on it. With the cost of paraffin and the smell we did without heating, and you could shake the dew off the bedclothes in the morning. When after a couple of months Alan moved out, I helped him in my Mini-van.

Alan and I have maintained some contact over the years. He was a bright, self-driven extroversive type who was always destined for mainstream fame and a place in public consciousness with his dynamism and charm. He was an intelligent man, though not an intellectual, with infectious opportunism and good humour.

We studied for three years at the gardens and both of us took our Diplomas in Horticulture with credit. He had a theatrical twist and we were both very fond of the written word. I'm told he went on to do quite well.

I confess to scaling the wall at Kew wall one afternoon to meet my young flame of the time, Susan Raeside, the daughter of a Harley Street doctor, John Raeside. We listened to the seminal sounds of *Stairway to Heaven* composed by the guitar genius Jimmy Page, and John and I used to study the work of Rudolph Steiner and talk about anthroposophy at his house opposite Richmond Park.

Tragically, in May 1972, John was one of the 118 people killed in the Staines air disaster. His plane crashed on take-off as he was on his way to a medical conference in Brussels. This awful trauma had a profound impact on our emotional life. Susan was overwhelmed with shock and I remember her clinging onto the physical reminders of her father, his bible and pen. My great friend from the Kew days, Barry Phillips, gives us his own account of this tragic event at the end of this book.

Sue and I parted to go to separate teacher training colleges. I went to Worcester College and qualified as a teacher in Rural Studies, which also took me to Malvern, Worcestershire, and Rugeley in Staffordshire.

During my studies we encountered Darwin, Mendel and other scientists of luminous intellect. That gave me an insight into theoretical genetics, and after sifting what I had learned I applied certain concepts to practical pigeon racing.

Although I hated the claustrophobia of London, I enjoyed shopping in the Kings Road in Chelsea, wore a velvet suit and a cravat and drove sports cars. My fellow students and I enjoyed an exuberant high life and some encounters with the psychedelic subculture. I encountered some great and influential characters at Kew. Arthur, an anorexic, worked in the quaint and lovely rhododendron dell. We sat on a bench and I shared his lunch pack up as he related his experiences on the hippy trail to Marrakesh, India and Kathmandu. Later, my own visits to those distant lands would open my eyes to the world of exotica, adventure and danger.

I soon tapped into the rich and diverse humanity on offer at Kew. Two Jamaican lads, Little Tom and Big Tom, were outstanding companions; they were laid back and laconic and made a beautiful contrast to the strident, assertive, compulsive and materialistic Westerners. Those boys exemplified the rich colour of a happy-go-lucky personality.

A character from the South West peninsula intrigued my naive curiosity with his cannabis plants, carefully tied, staked and cultivated. Bletsoe, Trafford and Tim Spurgeon immersed me in the rock and psychedelic subculture, culminating in mind-altering trips to the 1970 Isle of Wight festival. Alan, Mick and I, who were neophytes in the psychedelic subculture, set forth in great enthusiasm, crammed and laden with survival needs in a Mini-van. As we sped along down to the coast we attracted two young 'chicks' (as young women were often patronisingly referred to then) who gave us their sweet companionship in

Lymington car park. The island was electrified by the teeming masses of music freaks in a huge and wild musical organism. The locals were mortified as they watched the human dimension of the celebration take shape on the sun-charged fields. I recall the trembling effects of sunstroke and eating 'oggies' (pasties) fresh from the South West.

Although it was a drugs fest, we were loaded with the perpetual sounds of days and days of music as the stars of the day, including the Who, performed. When a mesmeric shaman called Jimi Hendrix performed, the crowd erupted in spontaneous worship. They had witnessed a twilight performance in the exalted career of the greatest guitar genius who ever lived on Planet Earth. Nothing else sounds like *Voodoo Child*. Two great forces of nature, the other being Janis Joplin, took performance art into a cosmic dimension.

I was metamorphosing from a sensitive country boy into a rather urbane young man – not before time. To my chagrin, a little narcolepsy sometimes interrupted procedures, as I would fall asleep on the seductive hot water pipes that warmed the tropical pits. Despite this I became an institutionalised and dedicated student, spending three years at Kew followed by a year

(1972-3) at Teacher Training College in Worcester, which took my total period of post-school education to eleven years. A daunting amount of hard work was involved, but by now I had a greedy intellect and an insatiable thirst for knowledge. During my studies we discovered Darwin, Mendel and other scientists of luminous intellect. I have since probed theoretical genetics, sifted it and applied certain of its concepts to practical pigeon racing. I have attempted to concentrate performance genes and innate potential by close inbreeding to performance birds in my strain over the past 40 years. By the same token I practise inbred/outbreeding to try and produce champions due to the surge in performance of hybrid vigour, as powerful genetic combinants manifest themselves in the offspring in racing progeny testing.

The dark side of this intellectual adventure was that I never stopped longing for fields, woods and hedgerows and flocks of wild birds, and the freedom to embrace the raw power of the wilderness. Yet it was all worthwhile, because it taught me to express my inner core in print, which has become an important element of my mature years.

Until I went to college I had seen very little of the

world, but in the 1970s I began to do something to put that right. My overseas travels began in 1971, when I was 22. A cool and charming Kew student called Tony captivated my imagination with his tales of his own travels, so one day in 1971 we set off from London in the little Mini-van on a quasi-migration to Sweden, by road. After pausing in Valenciennes in north-eastern France and being captivated by fireflies in the rugged outdoors of Belgium, we sped along the German autobahns, tasting the exhilaration of freedom. We were amazed that our little projectile still held together as foreign speedsters flashed by us. Sweden was populated by tall blonde folk who radiated good looks, especially under psychedelic disco lights in pulsating night clubs, and particularly the women. Tony and I baked on a beach in intense and dazzling sunlight until my skin started to peel painfully off. We savoured the strawberries in the garden of two blonde sisters, but no more intimate delights were in store for my friend, whose amorous efforts failed.

A few years later my anticipation soared as I joined Camp Africa at Asilah in Morocco and shared a primitive mud hut with a kind and seasoned old man of the world. A voyage of intense self-discovery ensued as we ventured far and wide into a new world. In Fez we saw the intricate work of skilled craftsmen in brass, wood and gold and the singular expertise of Tuareg nomads, the products of aeons of cultural time. The sights, the sounds, the smells were an opiate to the senses.

At the ancient tannery In Rabat, you could almost smell the vivid colours used by the workers who toiled barefoot in the heat to produce soft, high quality leather for demanding Western tastes. An evening in the pink city of Marrakesh dazzled our narrow little Western eyes with jugglers, charmers, dealers and a plethora of colourful characters.

Escaping the intensity and heavy city atmosphere, we arrived in the Rif mountains, breathing deep the pure air and scenic splendour. I found myself tasting hot sweet mint tea, a custom shared with the friendly Berber people. As fit young lads emerged from a rocky pool they held a cicada to my ear and I listened as it buzzed in peculiar and dramatic resonance. In the Kasbah I experienced cunning, ritualised sales effrontery as witty salesmen bargained for a living. It was an experience that would shape my young psyche.

CHAPTER 5

BACK TO
THE COUNTRY

In 1974 I found myself working as a zoo-keeper at
Drayton Manor Park in Staffordshire, in charge of
the birds. Life was spartan there as I was living in
a caravan with the chimpanzee man and a dog. The
chimpanzee man had a severe mental illness, and in
the end they took him away to a mental hospital. I
was sacked over a safety door incident with a harpy
eagle and was told I did not fit in with the zoo's

establishment and ethos. I overstepped the mark in that job, yet it was a wake-up call, a reality moment.

My days of residential education were over, but from 1975 to 1977 I studied Social Sciences and Humanities with the Open University. By now I had discovered the joy of poetry. In 1975 a flood of creativity came into my head and I decided to enter a poetry competition, the Eileen Berry competition, at the Guildhall, Winchester, and won third prize. I met with the intellectuals and graduate teachers at Worcester College and began to develop an interest in great literature, discovering William Blake, Dostoevsky, Kafka and Sartre. Perhaps the most illuminating for me was the profoundly mystical poetry of Blake. I still see Blake as the leading poetic genius of ancient times, yet his mystical psyche is nebulous to all but those initiated into the workings of deepest intuition and the unconscious psyche.

In particular I developed a fascination for Carl Gustav Jung, the great psychiatrist and psychoanalyst who founded analytical psychology, and read all 17 volumes of his work in York Library. I even used to sit and read Roget's *Thesaurus* page by page, as if it was a novel. I was fascinated by knowledge. Many outstanding personalities have since inspired me, and they include the Bird Man of Alcatraz and Nelson Mandela as well as the great authors and scientists.

Around this time I completed a course in hypnotism. The process of hypnosis relies on the hypnotist's voice, confidence, looks and overall charisma and the impact on the suggestibility of sensitive people if it is personality and brain based. Hypnotism can be akin to seduction and its use is well documented, as exemplified by Mesmer, Rasputin and Svengali.

⊱⋅⋇⋅⊰

In 1974 I moved to Southampton, where my parents were now living, to work in the parks there as a gardening chargehand. I also took jobs as a builder's labourer. Gardening and labouring are of course both very hard work, so I did not see this as more than an interim measure.

In Southampton I was able to return to my gardening roots. My appointment for the job with Southampton Parks by Terry Ball was bizarre, since I had initiated him being tossed into the bath fully clothed at Askham Bryan College. He was a slick and smart man who did not harbour a grudge. My work included The Cedars welfare home, a cosy, intimate little job where the matron was the mother-in-law of Mick Channon of racing and football fame. My immediate foreman was Godfrey, a total gent and a performing magician, being a member of the Inner Magic Circle. We hit it off, and I toiled and slogged away at hard labour. I was snoozing away in a shed when they came to promote me.

I remember Pete the Crook, whose scarred face from a knife attack reflected a history of burglary of posh houses, something he was proud to point out. We hit it off and he would pop into the bulrushes to smoke a joint at dinner time. A young and driven workaholic, I did three jobs – pool attendant, fun train driver, and chargehand gardener. Proud was the day when Pete and I walked into the showroom and I said 'I'll have that one', a Triumph Spitfire 1500 in topaz. We swanned around like two wide boys. In the evenings I was studying social sciences and then humanities at degree level.

By 1976 I had left my digs and was living with my parents, so when they moved back north to Yorkshire I went with them. This marked the start of a new age of tranquillity, and in the event I was to spend the next 30 years there developing a career as a pigeon breeder and racer. In fact I was never to leave Yorkshire again, except of course to travel.

In our new home at Old Sycamore Cottage, Holtby, I was once again surrounded by trees and open fields. Mother and I lived like spartan hillbillies while the plantation, orchard and gardens grew wild, but to me it was ecological bliss, with stoats and pheasants in the butterfly garden and a loft full of free-range pigeons. The plants form a canopy of total ground cover, in a diverse variety of native and non-native genera. The buddleia fed many species of butterfly, with hummingbird hawk moths, those stunning examples of convergent evolution, among the occasional summer visitors. My impression border, with florid nasturtiums and papavers, was intoxicating to bumble bees and other insects. Foxes, birds and hedgehogs loved it, and in summer the whole area hummed with the drone of insects. I have always avoided regimented, tidy plantings and adopted a let-it-grow philosophy. Insecticides and herbicides were banned, and the whole ethos was bohemian and back to nature, in pure love and respect of it.

We had many varieties of Narcissus, Tulipa and

Iris to study and admire. My garden was monasterial, a sanctum approaching Zen mindfulness. A creative mixture of native wild flowers, sweet peas, nasturtiums and gladioli bloomed in eccentric profusion.

By now my sister Pat had got married, to Roger Gilmore, and I became uncle to their two children. Their son Ian is ultra-bright – he is now a professor, Head of Knowledge and Science at the National Physical Laboratory in Middlesex, while Annette is a teacher and has a PhD in Physics.

At Holtby, I felt I was at last back in the wild, where I belonged. It was here I encountered a remarkable family of Romanies, led by Montagu 'Cocker' Smith who came walking along with his piebald horses and his bowtop caravan. Over the years we traded chat around the campfire smoking his Condor twist, and we gave them butter and cheese and a few racing pigeons as friendly gestures. I was impressed by the Romanies' free-spirited individualism, cultural traditions and ancient lifestyle. They lived in the bosom of nature, a hardy, spartan way of being, and knew the meaning of sun, wind, snow and rain.

One day Cocker asked me to overwinter his old English game fighting cock, a black and white bird of great spirit and the finest bird I ever looked in the eye. I put him in to join my other birds and he despatched my banty cock in double quick time. When I let the beast out he flew from tree to tree, crowing loudly. Then he sat on the cottage roof to announce his considerable presence to all of nature as well as the human community. Finally mother said 'Either you go or the cockerel does, which will it be?' So he had to go. Of course cock fighting is widely regarded as barbaric, and it has long been illegal in the UK. Nevertheless it has to be said that the old cock was an awesome creature of fiery and noble beauty.

CHAPTER 6

PIGEON RACING

Now that my years of constant uprooting and academic study in alien environments were behind me and I was settled at last in a home in the country, I began to nurse my vision of eventually building my own strain of pigeons. My intention was to become as good as I could possibly get. My mother fully supported what I did, contributing her own gutsy, competitive and aggressive attitude. In this respect she was a total inspiration and example to all. When asked about the secrets of her success, she would simply say, 'I sing to them'. She used to talk to the birds individually, and they responded. Who knows what is in the head of a pigeon? If anyone did, it was Dorothy. She was like Doctor Doolittle.

The first requirement is a loft, cree, shed, pen, or whatever you want to call it, to provide a house or shelter for the birds. Some of the modern-day lofts are very impressive, but I knew even back then that my pigeons would not worry about the décor. They simply require space, light, air and dryness. I believe it is better to be in the country for all-round racing from sprint to marathon level. Lofts in cities may give problems with controlled exercise periods, though they may be adequate up to 500-mile club and fed type racing. Wandering cats, neighbours and the dangers of free ranging may make life harder in a town as well.

I found a loft for sale in Tadcaster, and at £60 it was a bargain. It was old, and some joked that it would fall down as soon as the wind blew, but when the day came many years later to demolish it, it took 15 man-hours. It was 22ft long with door and air vents top and bottom and the birds had 'V' perches, box perches and plenty of dark corners to rest and hide in. It was certainly good enough for me and the birds. It was extended later, and as the shavings deepened my head got nearer to the skylights. The old structure housed all the race birds together, young and old, with the young birds tending to gather at one end for security (an image showing part of it can be seen on the Prestige Pigeons website). I was be able to watch the racers from an easy chair inside the cottage. On my open loft system I could muster between 20 to 30 old birds at the start of the season and 60-plus young birds to have a go at.

My mother had thought racing was cruel, as had my father, but I did not let that put me off. I had a vision for the future which drove my plans forward, and it would continue to do so for the next 30 years.

I made the overall decisions, while my mother's love and dedication to her son provided wonderful support. We made a formidable partnership. My mother was inspirational and like me was highly competitive. She was very tough and tenacious, and looking back, my achievements in the sport have largely been due to her. Her contributions showed that two united joint heads are better than one.

My mother believed in discipline and control

with birds and loft cleanliness, whereas I believe in an open loft and freedom for the birds at all times – I have found that freedom brings contentment and encourages endurance pigeons to home. She did not agree with my habit of giving birds away. In later years I was in a position to exchange well-bred pigeons with top fanciers such as Chris Gordon, Jim Donaldson and T. Robinson.

Living six miles from my loft, I worked out the easiest system imaginable that would favour the birds. Dorothy was an early riser and her first job, in her dressing gown, was to open up the loft, often as early as 5.30 in summer. Young pigeons in particular will fly well early in the morning. She brought a love of individual birds to enrich the atmosphere within the colony. She would sing and talk to them as they listened from their perches. This is the sort of love and attention to detail which encourages marathon birds to face it and return to the home where their wellbeing is so well cultivated.

In the early days I made the usual mistakes, such as pairing up too early, rearing too many YBs from racers, lacking a breeding and racing plan, sending birds to races on a 'willy-nilly' basis in the hope of winning something, listening to too many old wives' tales and training old birds too early and in terrible weather conditions. There are not too many pigeon men who have not trod that path in the early days, the product of perhaps too much enthusiasm, coupled with an impatience to go places.

From 1977 my father and I were racing under the name J and W J Emerton. He was very popular at the club and used to take the birds there in his little sports car. We all have to start somewhere, and I started my racing that year in St Lawrence WMC, winning my first young bird race with a little red hen. I can still see that little bird sitting and swaying on the wires for what seemed an eternity before entering the loft to become my first winner. In my first young bird race my birds were 1st, 2nd and 4th into York – I was hooked.

In 1977 I sent my first team in a very first Falaise channel race and was third with a Jack Ross bird. It was a baptism of fire and led me onto a tortuous path in the sport.

Back then the aim was to aspire to 500 miles on the day, and it took some doing with the feeding systems we had at that time. Old characters in the local clubs were celebrated heroes, men of power and distinction. My philosophy as an inexperienced new racer was to do my best, focus and progress, with the aim of getting all my birds over the Channel as a basic target principle. My birds mastered greater and greater distances and degrees of hardship, and how wonderful my first clocking on the day at Nantes NFC was with Damien at 466 miles, a feat which I repeated many times after that with yearlings and older birds. I studied the works of the scientists Pavlov, Lorenz and Tinbergen – all brilliant men in the field of ornithology.

In my youth, winning races was the be all and end all, and a great deal of work was devoted to road miles training. Now with the insight of age I believe most of this was surplus to need.

Soon after we moved to Holtby I met Jack Ross, who quickly became my mentor in the sport of pigeon racing. Jack kindly took me into his care and set me off with racing birds and got me into the clubs. It was he who in the 1970s enlightened me about the wisdom of being generous with one's expertise – and one's pigeons. 'Good pigeons are given, Jim' he said. I soon realised the essential wisdom of this statement, and followed Jack's philosophy throughout my career. Years later when I retired from racing I gave away all my birds, clocks, baskets, etc as a gesture to the fancy. I will be eternally grateful to Jack.

I began to read every serious book on pigeons. As a young man I read my way virtually around the library, with great satisfaction. And where pigeons are concerned, if a book yields one good tip, it is worth reading. Two books I particularly enjoyed were *Vets' Tips for Fanciers* and *Long Distance Racing* by John Clements. The former is a brilliant work full of scientifically-based fact and insight from five of the world's leading vets. Its international significance is underwritten by the famous Hungarian vet Zsolt Talaber.

One day in 1978, Jack Ross told me I was living like a monk, and in the hope of putting that right he took me to a dance at a social club. That was where I met Jean, and she proved to be the salvation of my life. I sent her to sleep with incessant chatter about pigeons and myself, but strangely enough she didn't seem to mind. I moved in with her in September 1979 and we have never been apart since. She is a kind and jolly soul and lights up the room wherever she goes.

In her modesty she has never craved publicity, yet she loves singing and dancing.

Jean had been married before and had three young children, Jeanette, Billy and David. We never had children of our own, but Jean's three made up for that and I have always got on well with them, as their friend rather than a father figure. They see me as a bit of an oddball, but in an affectionate way I think. She also got on well with my mother from the outset.

However, at the time when I met Jean I was planning to take some time off to go and see the Himalayas, and I was still determined to go. Jean was very upset at first, but she accepted my promise that I would be back. I was away for four months. When I came home I had long hair and a beard, and must have looked like a hippy. But I had a haircut and got cleaned up before I went to see her, and we have been together ever since.

In May 1979, while I was in India en route to the Himalayas, I had a presentiment. I told my companion, my American academic friend Joe Lemak, that my father had passed away in England. The impact was so great that I had to lie down. Soon enough it was confirmed that he had died. The funeral arrangements had to be made in my absence.

I continued with my journey and reached Kabul via a remote, rugged and epic route along the seemingly endless and soulless Khyber Pass. There was swirling heat, arid rocks and military outposts, but nevertheless it was a popular journey for tribal lords, drugs and every devious shade of humanity. Stepping with eyes open into primitive and ancient Kabul, eyes assaulted by open sewers, shanty and jostling tribesmen, I became aware of my naked and singular strangeness in this ancient and unique capital. Although there were celebrations of the communist rule, armoured vehicles alerted me to the military presence.

In Chicken Street in Kabul, transfixed by a seedy and shady rogue, I was drawn by intense fascination into a narcotic den. Unable to control an inner yearning, I bought a solid lump of opium, like a piece of black tar. Retiring to my hotel bed, I waited for the life-threatening, deep sleep of dreams, induced by that wicked witch of a poppy flower whose power is masked behind delicate blooms.

Anxious American traveller friends searched for the fading pulse and heartbeat; was the flower to claim another victim? Then the renaissance. I awoke light, euphoric, ethereal and empowered from within, to begin the journey back to life from the nothing I had become.

My photos taken with locals show that they were friendly, exotic and welcoming – I still have the gift of a fox-fur hat to prove it – and the raw taste of opium was uplifting in a very cerebral way. We travelled by ancient bus with no air conditioning, and by the time I had reached the Himalayas my mind, soul and spirit had evolved and morphed into a more enlightened form. The East has much to teach the West, and I try to apply the wisdom gleaned on my worldly travels in the now today.

We travelled by ancient bus with no air con, and by the time I had reached the Himalayas my mind, soul and spirit had evolved and morphed into a more enlightened form. The east can teach the west and I try and apply the wisdom gleaned on my worldly travels in the now today - sounds like a Shaolin monk.

This became the first of many adventures overseas, although there were no more alone or with friends; after that Jean joined me on my tours. While I was travelling I began to develop deep philosophical thoughts. At the top of a mountain above the Pokhara Valley in Nepal I felt so small against all that beautiful wilderness, and there was an enhanced feeling of consciousness. I began to realise that I had been brainwashed by the education system and conditioned to accept the ideas of others. From that point on I began to develop my own personal belief system fusing science and art in my own philosophy.

Back home, Jean and I both loved game fairs, country shows and terrier or lurcher events. My life was immeasurably enriched by her presence, particularly as like my mother I found she had a wonderful empathy and kindness with birds – the sensitive touch. She has a deep understanding of the daily practicalities, which balances my lofty intellectualism; the relationship works, and she even laughs at my absurd jokes. In the early days we enjoyed outings to train our birds and we would sit with Mum waiting for birds over many years sharing in the triumphs and disasters in the idyllic surroundings of the sweet cottage garden at Holtby village.

Some years later I wrote this for her:

Poem for Jean

You saved me from the shadows of hell
And plucked me from the arms of insanity.
Now I lie naked, warmed by your ethereal glow,
You are my beginning and my end,
A loving light in the eternal sea of love.
We are but one soul,
An unbreakable fusion into infinity, space and time.
Words can but hint at the wondrous place we now
share.

It is no secret that I owe Jean and my mother everything; they have been the nucleus and the soul of my career in racing pigeons, and the essence of my existence.

I soon found that an eye for the right bird is very significant in strain building. Knowledge and focus and a perception of quality and potential are important.

Incorrect training, mating racers too early or listening to ill advice can soon lead you astray. You need to gradually learn by your mistakes and try to perfect the system that suits you and your birds. In Holtby all my birds ranged as they needed to ingest grain, minerals and some vegetable and animal supplements. From 1976 onwards very few were shot, though some were taken by sparrowhawks. The female sparrowhawk (the females are substantially bigger than the males) is a deadly ambusher of racing pigeons. In anthropocentric terms she is cheeky, cunning and ruthless. In the 80s, my mother caught one with her bare hands in the loft. We would suffer many pigeon losses to them between late winter and April when the hens would sit in local woods. I confess it is very hard to watch a hawk strike a favourite down at your feet. Some of our racers became so alert that they were never caught, but Mystical Queen, Delta Lady and even Barcelona Dream were not so lucky.

The sparrowhawk is common in towns and cities, taking advantage of small birds attracted to gardens by the human love of feeding wild birds, and recently I filmed a male eating a blackbird eight feet away from me in my garden. We urgently need supportive legislation, yet this is very hard to achieve due to certain humans who instinctively covet, love and admire predators. It is a long, winding and difficult road to success.

My birds were pin sharp and almost wild, but they returned to the loft to nest, feed, drink and roost. Young and old walked the fields, sat on wires and sunned themselves on barns, and they were out all winter, even in snow. My mother and I would break the ice in winter if we had to, feed hoppers of pellets and supply all the birds' nutritional needs. Anyone may apply this to the right rural location after checking out local conditions. In my system all ages of birds were together on deep litter in the same loft at all times – a pampered, privileged free-ranging colony of pigeons. I still recall those days with fond remembrance.

CHAPTER 7

MENSA AND MENTALITY

It was in 1987, at the age of 38, that I discovered Mensa, and it became a turning point in my life. Mensa is a high IQ society open to anyone who can demonstrate a measured and approved score in the top 2 percent of the population. I applied to take the two-and-a-half-hour supervised test for membership, and recorded an IQ in the top one percent with a score of 154 on the Cattell test, which I believe is the same as Carol Vorderman scored – she is also a member.

The test I passed was the Cattell 111b scale, for

anyone who is interested. I rate it as the hardest cerebral challenge of my life, and it changed my world. I was suffering depression at the time, and my brain was super-stimulated on Amitriptyline, enhancing consciousness and self-awareness. Taking and passing the test was an extraordinary intellectual experience, and the result transformed my life from then on. It was a huge ego boost and confirmed my belief in my unusual ability. I love the exclusivity of Mensa; it is my home, a union of oddballs. Over the years it has become more diverse and better known in the media.

I now write for a variety of groups including art, literature, philosophy, ecology, conservation and autism, and I'm a member of 17 special interest groups and use their journals as an expression of my more abstract and creative ideas. I am also an advisory board member and I'm involved in a concept to mentor young and gifted people. I recently helped a young woman by giving her a little coaching to help her get into Oxford University.

As I 'age towards the sage' my membership means even more to my creative, philosophical and literary life. It is an effective cure for loneliness, and it connects you with some unusual and fascinating folk.

Around the world there are a number of high IQ societies, besides Mensa, such as Prometheus and Giga. All the members meet a standard criterion of selection, a standardised measurement. It is not an automatic measure of success in other avenues of life, or of other aspects of personality. Mensa has connections in many areas of the world, and I love my work in the special interest groups. The society is open to any person who qualifies. There is a tendency for intellectuals to be elitist academics. We must counter this bias with the pursuit of truth.

Mensa has institutions and connections globally, with far-reaching cultural influences both collectively and individually. Mensans are people with a diversity of social status, personality and interests. It offers scope for the insular introvert and the flamboyant extrovert alike to promote and cultivate perceived and measurable intelligence as we interpret it and understand it in direct linkage with human beings. There are abstract elements and deep personal qualities to its principles. I have no political ambitions to lead any committees or power-based hierarchies in it, regarding it as a vehicle for my diverse interests in philosophy, art, literature, poetry, creative writing, pigeons, travel and many other stimuli to my own brain – very introverted modes of expression, I feel.

I do not like crowds, finding too many stimuli in a group, and I feel threatened by the group dynamic. I prefer the company of one person at a time. My involvement with Mensa is through my computer, where I can contribute my ideas and thoughts to among others *Cognito, Science and Mystics, Scientists and Autistic Spectrum* and *Bipolar, Mensa Magazine, Cognito, Arcana, THINK!, Parnassus, Green Scene* and *Lyriq.*

Writing has become a way of life for me, and it is my personal way of giving something back to the birds and the wild creatures to which I have devoted my life. The whole purpose of my writing is to project what I see as the truth of my own experiences, combined with knowledge gleaned from cultural studies of the arts and sciences. It is rewarding when people find it interesting or enlightening, although some of the ideas are deeply poetic or philosophical.

The creative use of language is vital to my hungry mind. Since boyhood I have had a lust for words, a gift which has yielded great satisfaction. I owe a debt to the educational system, writing as I do now for ecology and conservation, academics, poetry lovers, creative writers, art and literature, mystics and scientists, all within Mensa, and publish in a poetry group. I like to reflect my special feelings and insights into the mind of man about what we really know and don't know about the world around us. The great writers mentioned earlier, giants like Blake, Kafka, Dostoevsky and Sartre, have inspired me, and I aspire to having just a fraction of their collective wisdom and penetrating insight.

Membership of Mensa has opened up a sea of writing possibilities for me in specialist newsletters and magazines, and I now indulge myself regularly in this. My thanks to all who take an interest in my highly-personalised writings.

With an eccentric or unusual presentation before a psychiatrist you can be labelled and medicated with ease. Many gifted Mensans with esoteric knowledge could be deemed to be bipolar. The creative world is populated by many who are thought, in archaic, conventional terms, to be crazy. I see them as part of the rich diversity of humanity. Perhaps it is time to reassess what an individual is, outside the confines of a narrow labelling system. In this sense people can manifest assorted traits common to many so-called types, eg bipolar, schizotypal, schizophrenic and genius. To get at or near the top in any pursuit, these traits are perhaps essential. Behind the personality of every great sporting champion is the beating heart of a huge ego. Yet conscious cultural forces acclaim people as legends, myths, icons and geniuses. These factors are generated into popular consciousness by the media. We have to thank the writers who celebrate and lionise them in the popular press, because without them and other media, star personalities would not exist.

Are there any Mensans out there in the pigeon fraternity, I wonder? In my pigeon articles, I express simply my own personal take, supported by some insight, truth and experiences in the sport. In the final reality we are no better than other people, and it is only a distorted ego that might give us the delusion that it is otherwise.

I am fascinated by the concept of the self. The self can be described as the totality of physical and non-physical characteristics that make up a human being. When we look inside our own heads we may have varying degrees of insight or awareness of a force, a presence, an intelligent entity which can be called part of the inner self, but I believe the full inner self is not describable or definable by verbal language. We have varying depths of insight and awareness and I see intense feelings, not thoughts, as the true echo of the inner, experienced self.

There is a perception that it is egocentricity which defines an individual self, and that in reality we are part of the great whole with no actual separation of individual beings. It is certain that language and thought keep us short of absolute reality.

We are all here for society to make vital judgements on us with the language and thought of the day. I believe that if like me you enjoy sitting in a creek throughout a January night with your fingers frozen to the gun barrels waiting for ducks and geese, then you qualify to be called a little mad (or a lot). I did many such things in my wildfowling days. I always believed in mind over matter. If you stretch your mind to the limit, it will definitely make you psychotic.

In my life I have been labelled both mad and psychotic, but at the end of the day we are what we are. Genius and madness are just words use by the outside to try to describe the undesirable. I confess that on many occasions my gifts have made me feel estranged from close personal contacts with others. I would imagine that creative people in history have perceived themselves as isolates.

I admire the TV presenter Chris Packham's eye for detail; he has admitted to having Asperger's syndrome, a mild form of autism. The suave, charming, extroverted narrations of David Attenborough are worldly in their global enthusiasm. Both have a fanatical love of expressing personality in relation to the natural world, and both are clever and interesting men.

A friend who had been sectioned refers to me as his psychologist and psychiatrist. I
listen to his fanciful ramblings and show him empathy and intuitive understanding. As a poet, I feel for his inner world, which may be real to him, and attempt to communicate understanding of this in my responses to him. With the bias towards clinical psychology and psychology, there is a real need for sensitive folk who can perceive the inner world of tormented and disturbed psyches and set out to relate to them in a therapeutic sense. I feel that some sufferers may gain

valuable insights into the truths and causes of their problems.

The field of mental illness and psychosis as perceived by society and the psychiatric profession is fascinating to me, and it is a very deep, fluid and subjective area which defies dogma and absolute understanding – a complex mind is a vast reservoir of depth. Some prescribed drugs may mask or induce madness – how potent is that?

Depression has become very common in our complex society and its symptoms may include low mood, anxiety, panic attacks, phobias, a lack of drive, excessive sleepiness etc. Repeated and excessive stress will produce psychosomatic consequences and brain burnout. I find that a regime of two walks a day in all weathers strengthens the immune system, lifts my mood and helps creativity. It helps to take a pragmatic approach, to seek out and indulge in what you enjoy.

Manic Depression Blues

A poem dedicated to all troubled souls who are gripped by torture.

Way down in my shoes, alone in my shell, I am under the spell, the hopeless delusion that all is well.

I try in vain to ease the pain, my little excuse for yet more self-abuse.

In the complex of my mind is a dark empty tunnel, my only relief from the vacuum of an empty being.

My light is dimmed, occluded by an empty cloud, descending on me as a death shroud.

Is this my fate, a life's journey, the final sentence, a prisoner of the manic depression blues?

CHAPTER 8

UNION MAN

Despite my increasing involvement in pigeon racing, the 1980s were a decade when work reared its ugly head. In 1979, when I was a gardener at Rowntree Park, York, Geoff Wood asked me to be a shop steward. From 1980 I was the gardener in charge of some of York's parks and I had reached the dizzy heights of convenor of all the unions in York City Council employment, for manual and non-manual workers. The hierarchy loathed my impact on the organisation, because I insisted on working on principle and from the social perspective of the rights, needs and desires of the working staff.

I would not see staff overworked, abused or taken advantage of. That made me many friends among the ordinary working men. Mick Towey relates an incident when a foreman gardener came to the gardeners' hut one day and on seeing me pouring a large quantity of brown sauce onto my sandwich he commented that I would be better drinking the sauce. I said he had a good point and proceeded to drink the sauce straight from the bottle. The sauce did taste better without the sandwich.

I relished the role, and in 1988-89 I led a dynamic and successful review. This entailed meticulous planning and negotiations at the highest level, but I succeeded in securing substantial pay increases for many of the workers.

I was instrumental in negotiating better pay rates for workers and also better job descriptions and conditions. This system was carried out by awarding individuals points on a grading system that reset their pay grade and working conditions. An example of this was that a working gardener in the glass houses for instance was given a new job description as Gardening Craftsman.

In essence the aim of the council and the Government was to downgrade the workforce and restructure the staff in order to save money. In fact what occurred was the downgrading of the workforce, meaning some people lost their jobs. Staff numbers went from approximately 150 down to 90 gardeners. But on the other side those that retained the jobs had better incomes and better working conditions. We both cost the council a lot of money in redundancy and wage increases and also in back pay for the staff that were retained. With this restructuring, one of the conditions was that there would be no overtime paid to staff for a period and that it would be reinstated at a later date, which it subsequently was.

The new system involved awarding individuals points on a grading system that reset their pay grade and working conditions. For example, a working gardener in the glass houses received a new job title, a gardening craftsman.

There were many back-yard meetings in order to resolve and plan strategies for negotiation, working closely with Mick Towey. This however was not supposed to happen. It also seemed to occur within the management structure. It was not supposed to happen there either!

After the negotiations were concluded and the 'reforms' were in place, I was given the new position of Head Gardener at Rowntree Park. I was followed within a year by my good friend Mick. He has commented that as an individual I sometimes had a problem with authority, and certainly where I saw inequality I would always challenge it.

Under the influences of the local council, I became aware of the obvious hierarchy, the power struggle and the systematic bullying which lay at the core of the institution. Wearing the red shirt of the left-winger I operated in a climate of hostility, aware of the need to protect my own integrity. The irony was that my job was on the lower rungs of management, yet l negotiated and made my presence felt in all the corridors of power. We had some notable victories. Feeling the cumulative effects of the stress of these years, I took early retirement from the rat race cauldron, having seen the ugly face of humanity in a hierarchical institution.

In the end, after many years of repeated toil, l

surrendered to stress and the personnel section, in its compassion and wisdom, allowed me to retire, so I was able to say goodbye to committees and politics. Committees are the natural habitat of people with social ambition, and I avoid membership of them all, preferring the lone wolf approach to self-assertion.

Jim Prothero told me not to let the morons grind me down, and I took this to heart. Since then I have been labelled in print as an eccentric, an icon, a genius, a lunatic, a manic depressive, a schizophrenic, psychotic, hypomanic, paranoid and many more of the contemporary labels favoured by society. In reality, as I introspect, I am just an original, whole being, a man who walks alone in life. It is true that there have been broken relationships and burn out with drugs, sex and rock 'n roll, but in the final analysis my books tell a true story.

Since then I have avoided politics at all costs. I have no time for the dishonesty of politicians, who I see as no more than con men. I never vote. I see democracy as an idealised, formalised and abstract phenomenon. My experience in leadership and the knowledge it brought me of the psychology of power in various institutions gave me an insight into how it works. Under the cloak and veneer of democracy, the elected leader often has an ego-led, careerist objective. Through subtle processes of persuasion and manipulation, many will rise in their positions until they act more like dictators.

I perceive that democratic politics is often laden with deception, as evidenced in the House of Commons, where the exchanges between party leaders are biased, polarised and propagandist, and lacking in truth and objectivity. Sometimes there emerges a democratic leader who is a visionary with real intellect and integrity, such as Enoch Powell. In leaders who don the mask of representing the people, a scanning electronic microscope with high-powered perception is needed to probe the truth. Beware the difference between ideology and perceived practice.

Back to my pigeons. One day I saw an advertisement by Louella Lofts for the Stichelbaut strain, and I knew from the picture that these birds were my future. They were of Descamps van Hasten origin, inbred to Alois, the Stichelbaut original of the 1940s, one cock being Darkness, the same genes as

The Tee, direct from Emiel Denys. There was also a grandson of the famous Van Wanroy Kleine Donkere, which had a legacy of winners at the distance, plus a granddaughter of Woodsider. I judged feather texture, balance and the total impression in my mind, having studied the evolutionary history of the strain origins and a montage advertised by Louella.

The matched pair selected from the sales pens were numbered GB 76J90513 and GB76J90079. They were lovely small dark chequers and I hit the jackpot with them instantly. They bred Iron Man and Iron Hen, parents of Dark Destiny, my no 1 foundation stock hen, and as brother and sister, when paired together, they produced my No 1 stock cock Dark Destiny and his brother, No 2. By inbreeding already inbred birds, I immediately achieved superb performances. Jean and I were hungry for success in club and federation races, and with time and dedication we made good progress and won a series of prizes.

On my little open loft system, in spite of losses due to nature, eg predation, most of my better results at Pau, 735 miles, San Sebastien, 737 miles and Barcelona Int, 879 miles, were achieved by hens – I found them more tenacious with regard to the nest and to have high survivability.

The memory of my little Dark Enchantment lives long and vibrant in my imagination. She was a little dark chequer hen inbred to my no 1 pair, Dark Destiny and Daughter of Darkness. She scored twice from Pau NFC at 735 miles to Holtby, arriving in the hours of darkness at 10.08 pm, hence her name, and was verified at Barcelona International 879 miles injured. She served my stock team well for 11 years. She was paired to a son of Circus Boy as well as to Barcelona Dream. Her genes provided many excellent offspring for Jim Donaldson and later Nick Harvey with 11th open BBC Barcelona International at 710 miles and Trevor Robinson with a 2nd in the north section BICC Barcelona International at 854 miles.

Dark Enchantment was recorded twice at Pau 735 miles and once at Barcelona 879 miles and she lived out her days in the stock loft. She is a bird I recall with great affection – a real old-fashioned marathon pigeon. She was a testament to marathon performance inbreeding, and her descendants have continued to excel in the field.

In pursuit of race wins at club and federation level,

Jean and I would take a flask and make a nice little day trip of it, taking in Yorkshire beauty spots like Filey, the Humber Bridge and Beverley. Sometimes we would try to beat the birds back home. The birds would be doing up to 1200 yards a minute, depending on the wind, the equivalent of 40 mph in a car with no traffic lights to worry about, so you would need to put your foot down to get there first.

We used local collective training facilities laid on by grand old Ted Booth, whose wife used to cook me bacon and eggs. We need more of these generous-spirited people today. For sprint training, we found that repeated tosses at say 25 miles on the assumed line of flight could do the trick. As I got older and developed more stamina, becoming distance and marathon orientated, from an open loft I began to enter hens at 95 miles and cocks at 138 miles. My intention was to condition the birds on maximum feeding for long international races later.

How long is a long race? I believe that the severity of a race depends on the human perception of it, and it's a variable concept. We can all conjure imagery of our most difficult race points and races across the spectrum of racing. Some 500-mile races are in fact more easily attained than 100, depending on the conditions. The beauty of racing/breeding are the unknowns, along with triumph over difficulty. It is often thought that races over 500 miles can be called difficult, and sometimes this is true, but not always. Pigeon racing beliefs are embodied by prejudice, myth and human personality – I am no exception. In reality international racing will always sort out your better birds of any named family or strain, a practice which I recommend following at least once in a pigeon's lifetime. In my experience of looking at the Barcelona International races into the UK, they all offer mind-bending difficulty.

My greatest bird was Diabolos, born to my no. 1 pair. In 1985 I entered him in the blue ribbon 516-mile race from Nevers in a north-westerly with a total of 2,516 birds in the Yorkshire Middle Route Federation. The old cock was on fire and shone like a diamond in the basket. That bird crossed the channel and clocked the same day. When he loomed low over the cottage on silent wings at 8.50 pm to top the Western Section and come in 6th open, I knew my distance career had begun. He would be given the Fed's best performance of the season trophy for multiple performances. In fact I stopped racing him at two years and he lived to the ripe old age of 22.

Diabolos founded a dynasty of good birds, including Mystical Queen and Barcelona Dream, of whom more later. In fact Diabolos, whose number I also still remember – GB 83S35305 – is my favourite bird of all time. It was the right bird on the right day that gave me my destiny in the sport – the essential final link in a long chain. Descendants of these birds are still scoring at Barcelona International.

The key is close family breeding to raise performance racers and breeders on winning methods. Thanks to Louella Lofts and the Ponderosa UK, other descendants of my first pair are still winning races today. The birds today are all down from the seven foundation originators, especially Dark Destiny and Daughter of Darkness, my no 1 pair.

Until 1992 I raced in club/fed events and opens. I found that it is difficult to be popular and a good racer at the same time; I have sensed negative human emotions from others and for many years I trained only in organisations before national/international races.

A bird needs two to three weeks' complete rest,

with no road training, before a big international race – its internal organs need to be lined with fat, like a swallow migrating from Africa.

I would enter birds tossed at 90 miles from all parts of the compass, and they did equally well. I would usually start training a fortnight before racing began. The old birds for national and international racing were trained by entering shorter races of the programme.

As far as we can perceive, the how and why of homing and orientation remain elusive to science as well as to the fancy at large. Who can tell what a pigeon experiences within its being or the exact impetus that drives a pigeon to home over great distances up to and sometimes over 1000 miles against variable weather conditions? it remains a beautiful mystery. Scientific methodology applies experiment and analysis in an attempt to resolve the enigma with examinations of sense of smell, ESP, magnetic fields, the sun, landmarks and other physical and non-physical phenomena. Having jumped birds over 500 miles into races, it is my belief that a bird may know or otherwise sense a homing impulse sitting in the transporter which may never be properly understood.

In my long career in racing pigeons, I never held birds at home due to forecast inclement weather conditions. In particular I liked north-east winds as a real test of management and bird and mistrusted birds with velocities over 1200 yards per minute. Many sprint/middle fanciers will disagree, liking the birds home sharpish and back under control – it is purely a matter of subjectivity and personality.

To fly 700-plus miles, a nice warm-up race of 10 to 12 hours was crucial in preparation terms and some birds will go 17 hrs on the wing. We do what suits us as individuals and I like birds to experience a holdover in the systematic preparation for international racing where long periods in the transporter are symptomatic of the race. My strain evolved over hardship. Such is the nature of the beast.

Sending to any race point is a journey into the unknown, with the birds at the cruel mercy of the elements. We may feel secure in our guesswork of the outcome, yet the beauty lies in uncertainty. Will we produce the rare champion, a strain maker to propel our name into the future? The race may test our mettle, our inner resolve, in our attempt to triumph over nature or be at one with it. In competition with our peers and rivals we have stirrings of a primal nature – will our ambitions be realised? As man conquered Everest, our highest aspiration may be Barcelona. It is a spiritual odyssey to self-realisation, a giant leap of faith into the future.

At that time in the 1980s the aim was to aspire to 500 miles on the day, and in those days it took some doing with feeding systems as they were at that time. Old characters in the local clubs were celebrated heroes, men of power and distinction. My inexperienced, naive philosophy was to do my best, focus and progress with all my birds going over the Channel as a basic test principle. After a long struggle, and in a learning curve my birds mastered greater and greater distances and degrees of hardship, and I well remember how wonderful my first clocking on the day at Nantes NFC was with Damien at 466 miles, an achievement which I would repeat many times with yearlings and older birds.

At that time Pau at 735 miles seemed like an impossible dream, yet ambition took me there with a leap of blind faith.

My mother Dorothy, aged 17

My father Walter James Emerton

A happy five-year-old Jim Emerton with Charlie Fantail and a young pied.

Jim at primary school in Skegness (front desk, centre of picture)

With my class at the Royal Botanic Gardens, second row, second right.
Alan Titchmarsh is just in front of me, front row, second right.

Jim with Ben at Alvaston (1967)

Jim with his first goose (1969)

Accepting a retrieve from Ben

Jim with a curlew on the gangplank
at the houseboat

Kenzie in the famous houseboat

Jim the hippy
in India

Jim in
Florida,
1991

With 'Dorothy's Courage', 1989

Yorkshire Middle Route, 1990. Dorothy Emerton at 73

Jim with some of the family

Jim and Jean out for a meal

Jim in his natural habitat

Jean in our garden

Cooneen Jane, the greyhound

Jim at a nursery

Jim at his York home

Jim with a Barcelona Trophy for
pigeon racing

Jean at Moorlands Nature Reserve

Mum helping in the loft

Mum at Sycamore Cottage with Champion Diabolos

Mum feeding tame geese at Warthill. Aged 91

K. Emerton 1994

PETER BENNETT

"DIABOLOS"

G883 S35305

Diabolos

J.C. Emerton
1994

PETER BENNETT

"DARK DESTINY"

GB78 S6321

The No.1 stock cock bred from Iron Man x Iron Hen.

The early Emerton Stichelbauts in montage.

Champion bird 'Dorothy's Courage'

CHAPTER 9

TRAVELS WITH JEAN

My success with the pigeons began to bring in money, and after I had settled down with Jean, we found we could afford to embark on a little travelling. In the 1980s we visited 36 countries and islands altogether, and I treasure many golden highlights from those years.

There are many occurrences in life that are beyond human comprehension even by the most sophisticated scientist. During my time in Delhi I encountered a celebrated seer. We met on a personal exchange in the grounds of a swish hotel, and he asked me in silence to focus on one word in the world of words. Writing something on a piece of paper, he rolled the paper up in his hand, then asked me if I wished to continue. In quiet and cool anticipation I said I did. He opened out the paper to reveal the word 'JEAN', the very word I had my mind focused on. Somehow he had read my mind.

On Lake Dal in Kashmir, we stayed on beautiful and exotic houseboats beneath the snow-clad foothills of the Himalayas. The air was crisp and pure and the sky was a startling blue against the white mountaintops in the distance. A lone eagle soared effortlessly above the snowy peaks. Below, beneath the pristine waters, four kinds of exotic kingfisher dived into the lake, and silver fish boiled in a feeding frenzy. I felt an inner spiritual metamorphosis as I began to inhale the cool smoke from a hookah pipe and the opium and hashish glowed and smouldered. That hit was life-changing for my brain and psyche, as I had a perception of my spirit dancing on a water lily that floated serenely on the shimmering lake. It was a pure, powerful and beautiful feeling to be liberated in that way. Then came a huge sense of flying over the lake towards the snow-clad peaks, somersaulting and touching hot red and cool blue with open hands, in pure ecstasy and disembodiment. How do we explain this in terms of the brain/mind synthesis, mysticism or altered states of consciousness? This and other experiences in life have shaped my perceptions, thinking and creativity.

We saw the lovely Sacred Ibis in its native habitat in the wetlands and fields of India. To see them in flight against the scorching sun is an incredible sight, as is the black Glossy Ibis. The sights and sounds, smells and colours enriched my senses and altered my personal perceptions of life. The exotic birds I saw in India on my travels to the Himalaya were a kaleidoscope of avian wonder. I saw a Roller Bird and a Malachite Kingfisher, a living jewel. Like the cranes of Japan and the Birds of Paradise of the jungle, these beautiful birds are as near to perfection in human eyes as can be reached by the natural world.

Our meals were prepared by a turbaned 'houseboy', a remnant of the Raj. With glowing pride he produced a reference book from the British officers he had served. He was a delightful and charming man. We took visceral pleasure in a wedding feast which included cooked water lily shoots. I confess to enjoying the cool smoke of a hookah pipe, and the consequence was extraordinary in a psychic sense. In Srinagar, the capital, I tried on a wolfskin coat and bought Jean an ornate papier-mâché jewellery box.

In Chicken Street in Kabul, transfixed by a shady rogue, I was drawn by intense fascination into a den of narcotic vice. My curiosity led me to buy a solid lump of the black tar of opium. Retiring to my hotel bed, I waited for the life-threatening, deep sleep of dreams induced by the poppy flower, whose power is masked behind delicate blooms.

In the Golden Temple of Amritsar we found local musicians absorbed by the resonance of sitar music. With senses intoxicated I gazed into the illusion of a magnificent hall of mirrors depicting far-reaching self-images.

In stark contrast we gazed from a boat on the Ganges at sunrise on the burning bodies of a sky burial, in spiritual purification. Vultures circled overhead, then swooped down for more pickings from the macabre remains. Our credibility was tested by a stunning girl who sold us a perfect lotus blossom for one rupee. The teeming masses of humanity before us were enthralled by the ancient and captivating conquest between mongoose and king cobra. In elegant tropical gardens, as streams of colourful parrots scorched the evening skies, we absorbed these memorable images in silent gratitude.

In the Pokhara Valley in Nepal, gently absorbed by gaily-coloured blooms, I luxuriated in detached reverie and gasped at the majesty of Annapurna overhead. Awestruck, I was made to feel tiny at the feet of those snowclad peaks, sensations that morphed my mind. I felt a complete loss of ego because you are so small against all that nature, and there was an enhanced feeling of consciousness. We mingled with Tibetan refugees, and I enjoyed their strange singularity of exile and the delightful Snowlands gin which they made. In Kathmandu a handsome, steely-legged rickshaw cyclist escorted me around the Nepalese capital, which proved to be a cultural explosion.

On a sultry evening deep in Pakistan, I summoned a pony and trap driver for a journey that would be life changing. To the clip-clop of practised hooves we trotted into the unknown and an appointment with fear. After a period of time thick with emotion we stopped at our secret destination. Drawn in by the occasion, we ascended a spiral staircase into what could have been the room of doom. Three men plied me with hashish and attempted to turn me into a narcotics mule, and sensing the possible ending, I asserted my desire to return safe and legal back to the hotel. This realised, my deep anxiety was suffused by intense relief.

In Turkey, in sight of Odessa and the Russian border, we marvelled at the Blue Mosque of Istanbul, surrounded by elegant minarets, a feast of beauty for an aesthete's eye. We devoured the delicious chocolate mousses tinged with green pistachios at the Pudding Club, that famous meeting place of travellers and hippies. We traversed the ancient Bosphorus in contemplation of the East meets West connection. I found the people to be generous and friendly, and the traders in the countryside left their precious goods out far into the sultry night, sure of human trust.

Witnessing the tourist trap of Troy of literary fame, we journeyed into the Goreme Valley to behold a lunar and rocky landscape with fanciful fairy columns and troglodytic cave-dwelling individuals. The scenes challenged perception in weird formations. We languished in the cool springs of the calcite pools of Cappodocia, reflecting on the earth's magnificence. In Dalyan we were purified by the silky mud as it cleansed our skins, later to relish the bodily embarrassment of steaming hot Turkish baths in the Hamman tradition.

In Malta we found little birds caged for their fragile beauty singing for their freedom from bougainvillea-clad balconies. We ventured into the summer night to relish the heady perfection of cocktails in Sliema. In the morning after a euphoric evening we found a street fish trader crying *'Lampuki, lampuki!'* and watched the graceful yachts as they floated serenely out of Valetta harbour.

We found the Rock of Gibraltar enveloped by dewy mist and saw the impressive forms of barbary apes or macaques. We became aware of the military connection, and of the fractious dispute in sovereignty between England and Spain, which still bubbles in the human cauldron today. On a lighter, more materialistic note we searched the crowded streets in pursuit of cheap whisky. A Russian influence in the form of a hospital ship lay in calm dominance offshore, conducting eye operations for the needy.

The clear and soft light of the Mediterranean was the visual medium for artistic greats like Matisse and Chagall, and I too find myself inspired by its beauty. We felt uplifted as we strolled arm in arm along the Promenade des Anglais at Nice, though the ambience was ruined somewhat by a jumbo jet which hung low over the sea. Under a sapphire-blue sky we experienced the sensory delights of Antibes and Juan les Pins, the stylish villas, their elegance framed by dramatic green conifer trees. The roof of one bore the symbol of John Wayne in the form of a 10-gallon cowboy hat, notable for its quaint eccentricity.

Our feelgood factor persisted as we searched the coastal waves in pursuit of buoyant sea birds lifted by warm thermals. It was tempting to feel the embrace of cosy euphoria under such sophistication. We paused a little in Cannes to feel the impact of the stars which gave the film festival its cultural significance.

Beside Israel's famous Wailing Wall, strange men in black whispered praise and subservience to the godhead of their fantasy, each note placed with reverence in walls of cold stone. The silence was shattered by yet another exploding bomb, a symbol of aggressive unrest. A poster of John Travolta welcomed us in true Western style to the Holy Church of Nativity, its spiritual past celebrated in gold. Old Jerusalem's ancient factions of troubled and war-weary souls echoed loudly from the monuments of the past. In Jad Vashem, the hall of names gave ghoulish permanence to the pain and anguish of the Holocaust. The biblical gardens of Gethsemane were not the luxuriant paradise of legend but arid rocks baking in an unforgiving heat.

In Romania, the oppressive heat of the scorching sun reminded me of the acute risks to fearless and foolhardy travellers. The jostling queues for bread in a land of some impoverishment reinforced my notion of social need and deprivation.

We were drawn by acres of sunflower heads as they searched skyward for solar sustenance. In a dusty village, dancing bears tormented by cruel masters performed in abject misery for human delight. Ruthless and cunning gypsy con artists seduced gullible tourists as they parted them from their money. The supermarket shelves were void of produce, apart from stark jars of preserves shrouded in dust. An old lady, face craggy with time and dressed in peasant garb, sold us her wizened apricots for a few pence. It was a land of material poverty, yet we were spiritually enriched.

In Tenerife, the land of the canaries where only budgerigars exist, we savoured the unusual and distinctive attractions. With the blistering sun scorching down from a pure blue sky, we felt naked, stripped of our Englishness, as we endured the exposure with the native people on this island made of alien black, volcanic sand. Finally we sailed out into cool sea air, escaping from the beach of torment. A thuggish local took a peculiar dislike to my symbol of Englishness, a travel bag, and taunted me almost to the point of violent remonstration.

In safer climes we enjoyed the brilliant array of exotic parrotlike birds in the Loro Parque of Santa de la Cruz, as they represented the nucleus of an international conservation collection. A cockatoo projected his well-practised tricks, savoured by observant children in the controlled arena environment. We found a vivarium of venomous snakes, where the banded krait from Thailand was fronted by a message which read 'possibility of recovery remote'. After a flood of excitement we enjoyed the green luxuriance of the tropical botanic gardens in admiration of the labelled and rare specimens in the collection. On a more physical plane we climbed the rocky and harsh slopes of Mount Teide, breathing in the heady, sulphurous fumes from the crater.

We became more earthbound as we endured the artificial and conventional atmosphere of the Playas des Americas resort, where we were grounded by touristic realism.

Conscious of the pristine elegance, the sumptuous and all-pervading wealth, we relished the high life and opulent sophistication of the Monaco principality. Here the rich and famous parked their Rollers and prancing-horse Ferraris with gay abandon. With egos inflated we waltzed into the casino, our eyes transfixed by the ornate ceiling, our hearts lifted by the James Bond ambience. In feverish and obsessive excitement I lost all my loose money on the gambling machines. We walked through the grand prix tunnel and could almost perceive the ghosts of the greats, men of history, like the charismatic and mystical Ayrton Senna, the Argentinian ace Fangio and the impish playboy James Hunt.

As we drove along the winding corniche, we reflected on the cultural saturation and the sheer aesthetic beauty of our surroundings, against a global backcloth of shanty and human degradation in third-world impoverishment. All that is needed to enter the fantasy world of reality for the neo-riche is a few million little pounds, never mind where they came from.

The island of Jersey is best known for Jersey Royal potatoes, whose real claim to fame is not their sweet flavour but the premium paid for early gathering. There were many scars, remnants of the German occupation during in a hideous and needless war. The delicate pink carnations of a show parade portrayed a warmer sentiment, further enhanced by the intricate and elaborate work of the House of Shells. A tall, dark and witty coach driver spun us round the island. His wickedly infectious humour entertained us. He aped the bellow of a randy bull to call in a herd of cows, to ardent applause.

In the zoological collection bequeathed to the island by Gerald Durrell, the rare captives appealed to my ecological sensibilities. We marvelled at the spectacled bears, the white Asiatic tigers and the prehistoric-looking fruit bats.

Jamaica was the land of hurricanes, banana

plantations and blue mountain coffee. I loved the cool nonchalance of the locals, to whom chronological time was insignificant. Jean and I sealed our romance with a kiss in a cool, pristine pool after climbing the slopes of the Dunn's River falls. In lush and verdant foliage we explored the gardens, where in sight of iridescent sunbirds and butterflies that coloured a gentle breeze, I was offered ganja by a handsome security man in a smart uniform.

At night we wandered into the depths of Ocho Rios, where our physical and cultural differences created a communication gap with the locals. Later we bathed in the warm and shallow waters of Negril, where we were distracted by a relaxing aloe vera massage. Taking tea in a grand plantation house, we were disturbed by recollections of the former murderous lady owner who had exercised her reign of terror in times past. In the setting sun we gazed with intense focus on a streaming flock of white egrets as they cut the sky to their nightly roost on paths set far back in historical time. Fearing for our safety, we avoided the street atmosphere of downtown Kingston and absorbed rhythmic music from Rasta souls in Montego Bay.

We wandered slowly on camels along the whispering white sands of the Sahara, where the air was pure and fresh and the light crystal bright. We saw a scorpion, one of the ancient survivors of a landscape where aliens were not tolerated. Later I sat upon a black donkey, and with a spirit as dark as his skin he bucked and weaved in a haze of dry dust in the corral. Then with total impudence he left the well-trodden trail to graze on allotment vegetables. To add to the hilarity, a colourful extrovert, complete with sombrero, was tossed off his mount to hit the ground in a chorus of laughter.

My finest ride was on an Arab horse, while my most lofty and majestic one was atop an ornate Indian elephant in exotic gardens in Goa, on our return from a jungle where huge tent spiders lived.

Magaluf in Majorca, with its seedy, Blackpool-style character, was anathema to my delicate sensibilities. Yet we enjoyed the taste of spiny lobster, in a dish created expertly by a courteous Austrian at the Old Vienna in Santa Ponsa. in a state of hyperexcitement, I danced down the street in neat white trousers. The aftermath was an allergic reaction to the protein in the fish, accompanied by intense night-time nausea.

More suitable to a soul with Taoist leanings were the open spaces, rugged hills and mountains of Puerto Pollensa. I recall the singular beauty of a hoopoe, and the brilliant ostentation of a male redstart. In Palma was an inbred and unique colony of pure white pigeons, all nicely habituated to man. Clutching one in my practised hands, I observed that the bird was host to the pigeon fly parasite. we found the people to be used to touristic intrusion and largely unthreatening to us naive tourists.

Venice was distinctive and original enough for us to explore its aesthetic delights on two occasions. Despite the architectural heritage of the Doge's Palace and St Mark's Square, my most urgent need was to feed the dark chequer pigeons in the square. Once I was satiated by the birds we joined the throng on the Bridge of Sighs, absorbing the unique sights.

Later we boated in swish silence under the practised hand of a gondolier. The great Alan Whicker would not have enjoyed it more, despite the pungent air from the water which tainted our nostrils. In the square we were captivated by a little man who explained: 'for six hours the lagoon give and for six hours the lagoon take'. Venice in all its cultural autonomy is at the mercy of the sea.

In Portugal's incredible heat we suffered the deprivations of a hot and crowded coach ride across the soulless Spanish plains, where my only claim to celebrity status was projectile vomiting in a local field, perceived by ghoulish onlookers. The physical appearance of Figuera da Foz in Portugual was a huge disappointment, with crumbling pathways and monumental derricks on the beach. The negative aura was relieved by colourful ethnic dancing in a suspended ring. We were not prepared for an electric storm which consumed us all in its sheer intensity. Forked, chain and sheet lightning turned the sky into a luminous glow. I said to Jean, 'Watch that red bulb now', just as it shattered. On a more homely level we tasted sardines grilled fresh and sweet on the beach with wisps of pungent smoke in the sea air. In pursuit of quality port we tasted the drink from the casks in Porto, a con perhaps as it lacked authenticity.

Monkeys are tricky little opportunists that will steal anything from a banana to a camera, and break off your car wiper blades. In 1995, after an adventurous drive through the jungles of Goa, we emerged into a clearing. There was a beautiful waterfall, cascading down rocks, and here in the rugged terrain of the steamy, jungle forest we were faced with tent spiders in their huge, silken lairs. Then a monkey troop emerged from behind the rocks and headed out towards our naive little picnic party. The cheeky varmints tried to take all we had, from cameras to cakes. It is easy to liken them to street urchins of the human species for their cunning opportunism.

As a murky mist loomed cool and damp over the Rock of Gibraltar, we encountered curious and playful macaques. Having heard about the 'young lady from the Cape with her Barbary Ape', it was nice to see these dominant creatures in raw nature. The animals are part of the symbolism and folklore of the Rock, and must be conserved.

Perched on a thunderous V8-powered airboat, we glided over the Florida Everglades. The air was alive with excitement when we spied the nostrils of a large prehistoric alligator protruding from the water surface. Yet they readily consumed the marshmallows we tossed to them from the boat.

The gazelles of the African plains are athletic and

elegant creatures that bound and leap like gymnasts in the blistering sun. A cheetah must call upon all its speed and muscular power to kill one for her offspring, in the ancient ritual that has endured since long before the dawn of man. The Grant's Gazelles and Tommies are lovely to the eye, yet many of them are destined to lose their lives in the survival battle of raw nature. These herbivores add colour and spectacle in the swirling heat and dust of a wide-open landscape. As long as man values the wonder and spectacle of wild creatures, they will continue to grace our horizons.

In Gambia we were transfixed by the colourful sights and sounds of many exotic bird species. On an early morning trek through trees and farmland, we found Golden Orioles, Green Tree Pigeons, Kestrels and Hammerkops. The habitat was vibrant and rich with many colourful lifeforms. Then my eye spotted the glowing red throat of a little Firefinch, aptly named for its intense colour. That morning is etched in my psyche, as everything made an appearance, right up to the aerial predators that soared over the forest.

Later we were rowed over the brackish waters of mangrove swamps in a pirogue which Jean had to keep baling out. I body-surfed in the white rollers of the sea, and walked past the vultures feasting on monkfish remains left by local women who dealt with the catch. A trip into Senegal was enlivened by Senegal Parrots and many cheeky forest monkeys.

CHAPTER 10

A BARCELONA DREAM COME TRUE

In 1993, at my second attempt, I sent two birds to Pau NFC which were both recorded in the Open result. These two hens, along with two more, secured me top prizewinner with old birds in the NE 700-Mile Club. This result was at my first attempt and went to my head a little. I thought to myself, where do I go from here?

In 1994 Diamond Queen dropped from Pau NFC at 735 miles, lighting up my mind and firing my enthusiasm. I was now fascinated and deeply impressed by the endurance capabilities of individual pigeons. Diamond Queen was 72nd Open NFC Pau, 735, miles, with nearly 6,000 pigeons. She was a lovely hen, superbly bred, but she did not leave behind any more good birds. Where to next, I asked myself?

The goal that now loomed large was the colossus which is Barcelona International at 879 miles. In any year, I would not expect even one per cent of birds to manage such a distance.

With mingled determination and trepidation I set out to have a concerted go at the last chance saloon, the dizzy heights of the Pyrenees. I considered Barcelona to be the ultimate challenge in Europe, and it still is. John Lyden warned me of the difficulty, as I was the furthest flying member in the BICC. He also generously offered to look after my birds at his home and during marking. The problem of conveying the birds to Kent was solved when I sent them down to John with Amtrak, five hens to a box and the cock in a single box. The cock was so big that he nearly filled it. Barcelona Dream's physical appearance was extraordinary.

Finally, a week later on the Friday, the liberation

took place at Barcelona. At the local club I had asked Brian Denney to strike my clock, since I thought this would bring me luck. Brian, from Strensall PRS, was a great flyer who put up good performances from all distances year after year. My words to the Strensall club were, 'I'm going to clock'. My mother thought it was not possible at 879 miles, being too far. 'It's just a dream', she said. It was certainly that. I realised the onerous difficulty of the return to Holtby, the epic flight, but I believed history could be made. I knew the audacity of the whole adventure would set me apart.

Things were looking ominous as the winds in the UK turned east and north-easterly. Bearing in mind that my home was six miles away in York, I had to camp out at Sycamore Cottage Holtby to wait for my birds, no sleep and nerves jangling. I had been killing fleas on Freddie the Jack Russell when I heard the cock drop onto the loft. He walked into view and I felt a mingle sense of awe, elation and wonder. I clocked him in controlled excitement. It was 2.50 pm on the Monday in hard winds, three days from the release. Barcelona Dream was the only bird of 20,936 clocked at over 800 miles that year, the only bird in the North of England in race time. To this day he holds the record distance in the BICC. In addition, two of the hens were verified, but Diamond Queen never returned.

I must admit that camping out and waiting at Holtby was hard. With a marking station nearer to home, I would have sent my best birds with the BICC. There were enquiries from Japan for his children, some of which are with the Barkels and one with Trevor Robinson, and his genes are now well spread.

Years ago I campaigned heavily for international racing with the NFC with a series of letters and propositions, and so it was that in 2004 I sent five pigeons to Dax in France at 687 miles with the International convoy of 17,526 birds. One of my birds caught my eye because she had finished with great speed at St Nazaire, 466 miles. She told me something that day. I nominated her on the entry sheet and in the single bird NFC lib.

On the second day of the race my mum, Jean and I sat out at Holtby. It was a pleasant balmy day in July. We waited with confidence and expectation, until she arrived from 687 miles and was duly clocked with no fuss, the furthest flying bird in time from 17,526 birds. That was the climax to my career and a lovely day for Jean and me. Such memories ignite my lyrical reflections today.

That result put me in the European International loft rankings. It was her second time at Dax, and Dax II followed on early next morning. I rate Dax International as a bit harder than Pau NFC. I live in hope of others in the North of England racing at Barcelona and await the first arrival on the second day at over 800 miles in the International. The Barkels had two sons of Dax My Girl, and Ian Dixon, who helped me greatly with my house and loft removal, had one. Ian flies as Dixon & Son and has tasted much success with the NFC up to Pau. He is a charming, good-natured fellow.

Dax My Girl was sent on her first large, white youngster of the year with three weeks' rest after 466 miles. She came to be 1st Section B, 4th Open in the single bird NFC. Happy days!

Waiting for Barcelona Dream at 879 miles in east and north-east winds was a triumph of hope over masochism, and the significance of this feat took years to sink in and mature. That epic endurance flight ensured the survival of their genes as I went on to breed from them. It takes a dreamer with a little lunacy to do these things, as well as good birds. Fanciers will always continue to stretch the bounds of possibility.

Barcelona, with up to 30,000 birds in the main race, is noted for its severe degree of difficulty into the UK and Ireland, and birds on the second day are always the exception, let alone the third. The Barcelona International, which is THE big race in Europe, has yet to be won in the UK. Can it be done, and who could do it, with what winning bird?

The Barcelona International race is a global spectacle in pigeon racing, with glamour, prestige and lots of kudos and money involved. UK studs are clamouring for the bloodlines of the key birds in the race. I was offered a house to clock out of Barcelona International!

After Barcelona there followed a heady cocktail of awe, exhaustion and marvel at the stamina and will of the birds to home to my little old loft. Now as I write with poignant reflection, I see all my races and experiences in the sport as stepping-stones in a rich and rewarding life.

I find it easier to realise your dreams in life if

you have clear ambitions, targets or objectives. Mine have evolved since childhood days. A clear long-term plan is useful with breeding and racing hurdles to be overcome. Realisation depends on personal circumstances, ability and temperament. You may wish to be a top prize winner, federation or national winner in time, with dedication. At the end of the day a happy result may ensue and that is a bonus, yet sometimes anticipation is better than realisation. A shrewd fancier will see that he sources or breeds birds of the right intrinsic quality for the task in hand. There is no magic formula for pigeon racing success other than a home environment and personal system which works. It may take an age before you get what you work for, which sweetens the taste of success.

I know men who must have the names of the day and collect birds to admire as if they were crown jewels – these are must-have people. The purist and the case-hardened racing man will use his lovely birds to test his prowess and perhaps to seek fame and recognition in true competitive racing. The champion will aim to perfect an overall system where results will be the parameter of excellence, not the joy of keeping a loft of nice birds. I find many keepers to be warmly sentimental and kindly, whereas the great racing men are tough-minded and goal-oriented. Perhaps I am a fusion of the two traits.

From 1982 on I started to sell pigeons to many characters from the UK and overseas for £60 each or more, shipping them out from Manchester Airport. One night I had an excited call from a Mr Chun Wing from Kowloon, who asserted that he wanted some birds pronto. In my enthusiasm I bought an aluminium container, made all the arrangements and set off to Manchester in a rainstorm in my blue Datsun Cherry. All the cars had pulled over apart from a Porsche 911 in front of me, whose lights I could just make out in the misty, rain-splashed murk. I handed over the birds, and some time later Chun Wing rang me to say, 'Your pigeon no lay any egg!' And yet he duly bought some more.

I recall when Dr Tim Lovell turned up in his nice Jaguar in pursuit of children of Barcelona Dream. Acquiring two, he indicated, with nonchalance, the figure to write on the cheque. Then, placing them neatly in a tidy two-bird basket, he coolly passed me the fob to the boot of his shiny Jag. A delightful man who did great hospice work and was an exemplary figure in north-east pigeons.

Most of the really expensive deals involve China or Taiwan, where these birds are highly prized. Some of these birds have been sold for hundreds of thousands of pounds. In 2013 the Belgian breeder Leo Heremans sold his entire collection of 530 birds for 4.3m euros. Earlier this year (2019) a single Belgian bird, Armando, was sold to a Chinese fancier for 1.25m euros. Now retired, it was said to have a race record that had never been matched by any other pigeon.

I believe the greatest moments of a man's life in pigeons are priceless. Money may buy you some well-bred birds at inflated prices, although good birds are available as friendly exchanges on gentlemen's terms. To me humanity is greater and of more value than currency in a capitalist society. However if you want money, the Chinese will cater for your every need via shrewd and slick advertising of apparently really good pedigree pigeons.

There are some men of acumen who trade in fashionable names, when the irony is that each pigeon is an individual under the umbrella of a strain name. Although as Jack Ross said, good pigeons are given, it is wise policy to finance your expenses with a few sales, although I know a man who stands by his kind generosity and gives them away. In the vast infrastructure of modern racing in Western society the fanciers blessed with ability and dedication will prevail with their clever management of good birds, and they will all be different.

In 2002 Stephen Wain from Foston, Derbyshire, made contact with me. He had serious long-distance aspirations up to NFC Tarbes. I supplied him over the years with top genes from the family, some free and some for a song. Evolving from these was his No 1 pair of directs bred from an inbred son of Diabolos paired to Velvet Destiny, direct from Mystical Queen and Dark Velvet. The son of this pair became a key producer when paired to a red hen of Dark Enchantment and Circus Boy genes.

Steve has given my friends direct children of the top pair, and children of his three times Tarbes hen, an NFC section winner at Nantes. The latter is the dam of Nick Harvey's current No 1 stock hen, a champion progenitor to BBC Barcelona International level.

Nick Harvey and I became friends in 2009 when he wrote me a letter asking for help with marathon racing. Out of this a fine partnership soon developed. Nick, who works as a hospital porter, is a few years younger than me. He rings me daily, and with my help he has emerged as a great fancier of repute up to Barcelona International level. In the process we have transformed our lives through the partnership. Nick is touched by eccentricity and genius, which makes us wonderful friends.

In 2013, Nick and I had conceived and pre-planned our new assault on Barcelona International, the unrivalled and peerless race of all races. We set about the meticulous preparation of our seven candidates, comprising our total old bird team. I have already said that I find anticipation better than realisation, and an intense vigil preceded the final liberation. Barcelona involves total mental focus and the application of scientific techniques with intense underlying breeding of the birds. At 710 miles to Taunton, we needed one on the second day – quite a challenge to manage this to the west of England, as the cognoscenti will realise.

In blistering heat and from a north-easterly air flow we timed Musgrove Addiction on the 3rd day to be 11th BBC National. In a race of attrition we were pleased to clock another bird to complete our attempt at excellence.

We set out to cover 100 road miles in an easterly direction and liberated the young birds on their own. It was to be a calculated third and final toss for the birds in pleasant flying conditions, although over some towns and cities with tempting ferals and racers to zoom into. After four hours we had four birds and after 10 hours, 16 birds. The next day a further 17 returned after a night on the tiles – old birds always take time out.

In June 2015 we trained a team of 22 birds in the BICC Poitiers race and had 12 on the day up to around 14 hours on the wing. They arrived to peanuts and Supersix by Vydex in the water to restore them. There were seven yearlings at the distance (344 miles).

It tends to be a real test into the West Country and we are pleased to get them home on a fairly difficult day. We do like the organisation of the BICC and its excellent programme. We timed two on the first day with two more just behind, then a steady stream of birds arrived between 8 and 14 hours on the wing.

A racer flies on its brain/mind synthesis, a mysterious phenomenon not understood by humanity. This trainer has set the good ones, those with navigation ability and stamina, up for the future. Soon the birds will be treated and allowed to moult and grow for the rest of the year. The jump from around 60 to 100 miles disproves the theory of orientation/navigation by perceived or known landmarks.

Behind the mask of champion pigeons, the whole sport down to the writers, the scientists, the politicians and the rich diversity of humankind, is the hungry need of the individual mind. We may function in organised groups, committees and societies, yet these are only there to serve the individual needs of people. What do you covet? Is it money, fame, prestige, personal satisfaction, or an obsessive urge for perfection in your chosen sport? In the rich and colourful tapestry of man, there are some folk who act as ambassadors, patrons, mentors and philanthropists, who generate feelings of sympathy. I like the egotistic-altruistic approach of those who do real practical good. If you accept the premise that we are in the game for self-enhancement, where do you fall in relation to the unique and singular face of pigeon people? I am acutely aware of my own ego. Are you?

In pursuit of better and better performances up to Barcelona International level I have established a social and competitive network in the UK, from Cornwall to Holy Island. Quality birds are being provided with a common objective of raising standards in breeding and racing with the accent on strain development and the acquisition and application of gleaned knowledge via the medium of science and the art of pigeon racing. This does not have the formality of a club or society and the common ethos is excellence and the development of the racing pigeon. The network is provided on a spontaneous and intuitive personality level.

The great racing men orchestrate success with their birds in a structured and clinical manner. Having evolved and created a winning system, they target future races with the best of their birds. With insightful judgement the clever fancier will specialise in and cultivate the racing condition of birds with innate potential, whilst producing the team to optimal readiness and suitability to the tasks in hand. If he is fortunate he may hit on a champion performer, ie one that proves itself to be at the top of its class. I have noticed that outbreeding of highly inbred lines sometimes does the trick, and wise men practise this in the stock loft. There is no exact science or art to pigeon racing, but the champion flyers know the game and often replicate good performances, sometimes at a high level, eg Snydale Express for Chris Gordon. It's all a lot of fun and will engage minds for a lifetime.

In my specialist marathon racing, I would predict and plan around individual pigeons for years. An example would be to earmark yearlings that have flown in races around 500 miles for later 700-800 mile racing. This type of philosophy takes huge focus and dedication, yet can be very rewarding in national and international racing up to Barcelona.

What motivates people to dedicate themselves to so many years of hard work with their feathered charges? You need a dream, a vision of what you desire to achieve, or to win, perhaps against the odds. This may be suffused with an obsessive inclination towards perfectionism. A love and a deep understanding of birds may be the key to the whole process. Excellence in the execution of any sport or interest is fuelled by the brain. In my obsessive and fanatical pursuits, I am fed by passion and emotion. To be creative it is helpful to tap into and shape the contents of consciousness. The pilot in the process is the self-conscious ego. Extroverts especially may find this introspection alien. Apparently around two-thirds of Mensans tend towards introversion – I can see why. I have been able to maintain a Zen-like concentration in my interests over very many years, in an attempt to reach perfection.

I still celebrate the traditional philosophy of men who wait in desperate anticipation to feel the thrill of arrivals from great races and mind-blowing distances. I like the spiritual quality, the lofty idealism of it all.

I must mention the great Martyn Mitchell, an outstanding individual, now a millionaire in Belgium but who used to live at Wiston, near Selby. At his home, surrounded by Aston Martins and Porsches, was the most amazing pigeon-racing establishment I have seen. Over tea he explained some of the intricacies of his racing methods. No stone was left unturned in the pursuit of excellence, and could he race a pigeon! To be honest, he was in a different league. He returned no fewer than five birds on the day at MNFC Bergerac, flying 623 miles. An expert at middle-distance racing, Martyn has conquered the racing in Belgium. He is a man ahead of his time.

On the intellectual front we have the great Irish writer Liam O'Comain MA, who is a lovely, warm man with a romantic and spiritual turn of phrase. In his many writings, especially about marathon racing, he has informed, enthused and enlightened us about the great racing men of the past and present. His body of work secures his place in the future consciousness of the pigeon culture.

We all remember Derek Cutcliffe, the ex-naval captain who single-mindedly changed the face of how we perceive the hours of darkness, giving the RPRA a model for its calculation. Derek would indulge in some extroverted and heated letter debates in the fancy press and made an impact cultivating and selling his birds, including Stichelbauts and Van Hees.

On one holiday Jean and I found ourselves at Lindisfarne (Holy Island). I found the remote and rugged beauty to my liking, far away from the teeming masses of humanity. Near the coach park we spotted a nice little team of racers flying about, and after careful observation we found their loft. In the farmyard we were met by local fancier Jim Patterson, who, with ease and gracious hospitality, showed us around the lofts. Jim had a hen which had flown Bourges seven times, a distance of 620-plus miles. We exchanged details and remained in touch. It saddens me that today with modern feeding and birds the furthest distance flown is usually Bourges, there being no races over 700 miles.

Though pigeon racing has its feuds and its rivalries, I don't believe I have ever made any enemies; I can only think of two individuals who 'fell out' with me and that was only for a short time. The old cliché is true – you cannot please all the people all of the time.

In my years of writing on the world of pigeon racing, I have revealed all to the fancy at large. In my youth I was as selfish as I needed to be to realise my objectives in breeding, racing and selling. After a good run, and with age, I contemplated the fact that the sport was a greater concept than mere dominance in racing. There is the human and personality side to it, the promotion work and the teaching and intellectual sphere. Writers contribute to the creative and imaginative side of literature. The selfish man keeps his secrets and knowledge of, say, feeding and supplementation to himself, like guarding the Holy Grail or the elixir of life. Beware of shallow little reports in the media and filter what you are told, as it may be nothing more than bovine faeces. I believe only what I prove to myself. Although like a moral imperative I act as a mentor to some friends in the fancy.

Learning that all birds must be tested, we send the team to each preparatory race in the BICC/BBC and NFC before Barcelona International. This gives the benefits of variables like race points, transportation, geography and type of birds in each convoy. The weekend of our big race we empty the loft of all fit birds. Although anxiety-inducing, it has been rewarding over time and it certainly finds out the good birds and the elusive champions.

My advice today is to spend as little money on buying pigeons as possible. It is very difficult to pick a good pigeon on looks alone. Many fit racing pigeons handle with symmetry, silky feather, balance and eyes that sparkle like diamonds in the perception of the mind of the beholder. The flying world is full of strags like these, but are they any good? It's easy to fall for good looks in a bird: the sparkle in its eye, the balance, the symmetry, the feathering and overall physicality or phenotype. But most of these beauties flatter to deceive and are next to useless as breeders and racers. I place the greatest emphasis on the ancestry of the bird and believe there is no substitute for creating your own bloodlines, rather than trying to throw money at untried birds just because they look good. Nick and I take late-breds for stock from our best performers, which will be related to intensify and maximise racing performance potential. Beware, be careful, keep your money in your pocket.

I like a nice comfortable loft for the birds to come home to. It should be a cosy refuge with deep, deep litter and lots of nooks and crannies for shelter, security and nesting. You want lots of air space and width for good ventilation and to maintain an even temperature. The atmosphere should be calming and restful and it must be free from pests and predators. I like the birds to mate as they like and where they want in ample boxes. The key word is freedom, which generates contentment.

It took me many years of painstaking mind research with periods of inspiration to create a system that would produce birds that performed at a high level. I learned most from established experts and academics in the field of pigeon management. But however confident you are of your system, you will be awake in the night during the big races, particularly the internationals. Be careful not be asleep for the arrival of your top birds – I literally used matchsticks to prop up my eyelids for marathon races.

The most valuable contribution is the dissemination and expansion of top strains and bloodlines for the future benefit of the sport. However, there is a rampant and insidious malaise in our society, epitomised by the attitudes of some fanciers. I think it lies in the propaganda and negative perceptions of the messages in the media, and is a response to some of the personalities who govern our quasi-democratic society. At the core of this problem in the sport is an unhappy synthesis of commercialism, jealousy, criticism and a decline in generous, spiritual and moral values due to the unhealthy rise of materialism. People demonstrate their instincts and emotions in a diversity of guises, and the obsessive will to win at all costs is contributing to the rejection of balance, fun and enjoyment in favour of exaggerated hype, self-delusion and illusion. Bring back the long-distance master, poised in vibrant expectation, for the arrival of his old favourites in beautiful and kind surroundings.

In my long career I have realised many things. Here are some of them:

You will breed few really good birds and champions are rare, even if the parents are very expensive on the pocket.

There are no pure strains of birds.

Sustained inbreeding does work, if you have the right birds and know how to do it.

The person to put faith and belief into is yourself, not the rest of humanity.

A racer that comes good or is consistent may one day fail to return.

Some versatile pigeons will score right through the programme. A strain of pure sprinters or distance performers is an illusion or a commercial concept – they are all mixed.

Marathon races over 700 miles are usually much more challenging than sprints.

The most rewarding aspects of the sport are teaching/writing and the creation of a strain.

Race day is the real test of my management, birds and conditions.

I believe in giving good birds away to help others and the strain.

However good we think we are, we are but specks of dust within the vastness of the cosmos.

CHAPTER 11

PIGEON MAN AT 70

The last decade or so has seen some major changes in my life. In 1996 I began to care for my mother, who at 82 was in failing health. She stayed at Sycamore Cottage while I drove from York each day in all weathers. She continued to help with the pigeons for the rest of her life. She died in 2005, aged 92.

The following year, on April 4, 2006, I sold Sycamore Cottage and Jean and I moved into a bungalow on the edge of the countryside on the outskirts of York. I retired from racing the same year, and donated all my birds to the National Flying Club. Since then my involvement in pigeons has mainly been in writing about them for the pigeon racing papers and magazines and later the Internet. I have now been writing daily for almost 18 years, producing eight books and thousands of articles and poems for publication. I write for magazines with global circulations, one based in Canada, and I also write for the Kew Guild Journal. I conduct interviews and give them, and I write for many Mensa journals. Mensa has opened up a sea of writing possibilities in specialist newsletters and magazines.

I have not left the world of pigeon racing behind. My great friend Nicholas Harvey of Taunton, Somerset, whom I got to know when he wrote to me asking for help, has become a great racer and I take a keen and daily interest in his successes. Nick is a huge and entertaining character, and with my help he has enjoyed some wonderful successes. Nick and I send all our two-year-olds to this task to find out in the cold light of reality how good they are. Our selection criterion is returns in race time. As a simple plan we take late-breds off these birds for breeding, with the aim of a gene pool rich in winning genes.

The yearlings go up to around the 540 mark, eg Agen International or NFC Tarbes. This plan is purely for experience and as a stamina test coupled with orientation/navigation ability. We are less motivated by the urge to beat people, being in love with an abstract concept of the mind.

I feel we have to find a way to stimulate collective interest and knowledge of the sport. The people make it what it is on a global level, a fascinating, thriving and absorbing activity. I like to push the boundaries of possibility, to set arduous standards for my birds and myself in breeding and racing. The diversity of human characters I have encountered colour my imagination with memorable images. Perhaps my greatest contribution, made possibly by my insights and perceptions, has been my findings on the psychological and physiological behaviours and needs of the birds to condition them for marathon racing, epitomised and exemplified by the Barcelona International races.

Where would we be without the innovators, creators and people of distinction in the rich complexity of the sport? Real progress in systems, science, technology and the ethos of the sport are all based in the psyche of individuals. The mainstream is formed by acceptance of eccentricity into the collective consciousness, and the pulse of popular society. To personify this abstract concept, who is making an impact now? The marathon men and the exemplars of international racing are laden with celebrity juice, and described in pigeon literature, where they inhabit folklore and perceived history. The early pioneering days of the BICC are now cemented in the masonry of a beautiful and thriving institution of potential brilliance for purist international racing, orchestrated by the old guard of the collective committee. In the early 90s, I saw the early stages of the evolution of Barcelona International as a huge target and concept and, believe me, there is nothing in racing like timing out of a race which is greater than yourself.

With modern publicity more and more people are setting a Barcelona International trend, and having flown all stages to Pau 735 miles and San Sebastian 737 miles with success, I felt that Barcelona International at 879 miles completed my set of ambitious, slightly mad achievements. It is best suited to diehards who are stimulated by such tests. Many see the epitome of racing and their personal zenith as Tarbes, and the NFC interests us for yearlings, yet I feel the premier races in the club programme should be of an international nature, with much larger birdage, scope and radius. I base my ideas on having raced both Dax and Barcelona Internationals to Holtby. I feel the essence of our continued discourse is one of individual personal expression, a quality common to the whole of humanity, and may your personality go with you.

The ancestry of racing pigeons is so old and complex that the racing potential of any bird is difficult to predict, even with intuitive leaps or logical analysis of the flock. Apples may fall far from the tree, which feeds the uncertainty of results, and that is the beauty of the game, since with absolute knowledge we would not engage in the activity. Show me a pure selection theorist prior to the race lib who has become a racing icon. After 62 years in association with pigeons, I know little other than my own enthusiasm. Natural birds, contrary to widowhood myth, are still, with clever management, excelling in races, which demands a rethink about why. The sport, contrary to the popular stereotype, is in numerical decline, yet it is thriving, especially in the hands of fanatics and purists, and I do feel that in the UK the BICC heads the field, mainly due to its organisation of international participation and diverse national programme. Myths are formed via persuasive and iconic people in the pigeon popular culture, when my nature is to believe only what I have proved for myself.

I am still driven and preoccupied to improve my work as a writer, our performances at Barcelona International, and my overall contribution to the sport. Motivated by life itself, I still wish to improve, and set myself near impossible targets of achievement.

My advice to all is to spend as little money on buying pigeons as possible. It is very difficult to pick a good pigeon on looks alone. We live in a greedy, money-based world and everywhere people are out to make money out of you.

I will always value the educational establishments of Kew, Worcester College, Open University and now Mensa, where some great minds have influenced my career. Yet my real education has been life itself, as experienced on my worldly travels. The exotica, the sights, sounds and perceptions of beautiful and strange things and experiences have been mind and soul fuel for this earthling. The vast diversity, the florid brilliance of my little life, flood my memory. The deep and dark complexity of shadow time, balances and helps shape the psychic whole, the pulse of my life on the ocean of being. I recognise law, order, moral, religion and virtue, yet feel invigorated at times by a sense of personal freedom - we can conform yet be free spirits in the material world.

I am somewhat aloof in a philosophical, existentialist way. I like to meet people on my own terms in the outdoor environment. I'd be in my element if I could meet intellectual people out in the field. I have never been one to stay indoors and I still don't like buildings, still less cities. I don't go to pubs and I drink Benedictine liqueur, not beer. I like free, open spaces, preferably enlivened by lots of wildlife. Now in 2019 I walk 15 miles per week.

Sadly my sister Pat is no longer with us – she died in 2018 at the age of only 72. She was a creative, verbal and sensitive person, and I do miss her.

As I embark on my eighth decade, I am fascinated by the realisation that I have no real knowledge, as all of it is human-based and educational. Real knowledge is understanding that in an absolute sense we know nothing. I like to philosophise, to talk in an abstract sense. I like to think about cosmological theories. I sometimes look at the stars for inspiration.

I have studied Eastern philosophy, Buddhism and Darwin. For sheer intuitive perception I prefer William Blake, and I admire Thoreau's *On Walden Pond, The Lesson of the Moth* by Don Marquis and *The Glass Bead Game* by Herman Hesse. I like lyrical works – Dostoevsky, and Kafka's Metamorphosis, but especially Jung, who examined himself.

As a poet, I find most exchanges with people to be shallow chitchat, with some more meaningful exceptions. A poem born deep within the psyche may tap complex inner feeling states. I find this a great pleasure, sometimes euphoric and satisfying if the imagery is original. I hate common cliché and the collective ideas that are the lifeblood of convention.

I am well aware of the mistrust and duplicity of the man behind the mask, the Janus face of society. With a shrewd eye you can hope to see who's who and detect the reality behind the actors on the stage of everyday life. Seeing is believing, and I am astute enough to trust only what I know to be true, having filtered out what I see, hear and read. Some of the politicians are Oscar-winning performers in the theatre of propaganda. When you have travelled to the roof of the world, you can spot the chicanery in an instant. The corollary is that it is so refreshing to communicate with a person when for a while they remove the mask and reveal the truth.

I am still driven to improve my written material, our performances at Barcelona International, and my overall contribution to the sport. Motivated by life itself I still wish to improve, as I set myself near impossible targets of achievement.

I have travelled around the world, studied, meditated, examined belief systems and philosophical thought processes and have made a few insights as follows. Humanity does not know the nature of the intrinsic reality of the cosmos. Science, philosophy, religion and other human processes are based within the individual and collective consciousness of man, and within the limits of language and consciousness. In the vastness of the cosmic space-time continuum, a supernatural omniscient entity may exist, and I am happy with the idea that it does or does not.

Humans, and possibly other sentient lifeforms, can inject any meaning they like into the mutable perception of an external world and all without dogma are relevant to the individual being. To my mind's eye we are on Planet Earth to exist and live out a lifecycle and discover the inner man or spiritual aspect – ourselves. I require no further meaning or understanding than this rather solipsistic insight. Philosophy is a nice little teaser, yet we are all less than specks of dust, mere minnows in what is in here and out there. In the last analysis, I am without care.

Alone in the garden, as the crows loom large in twilight skies, I breathe deep on the pipe of dreams, my trusty briar. The midges bite, while the moths evade capture and instant doom at the claws and teeth of the hunting bats which have emerged from their ancient roosts. It is the haunt of patient and visionary men in a silent quest to realise dreams when the air will come alive with pure moments of magic.

I am alerted from my trance when a single old pigeon zooms in from distant lands to turn the old man into a folklore hero and sporting legend. History is still being made in the secret gardens of racing men who come alive in the magical hours of twilight.

A LIFE AFTER PIGEONS

Abridged from a 2006 interview with Les Parkinson
(reproduced with permission)

When I have had reason to call Jim in the past, I have found him to be a little reserved. However, now that his pigeons are gone, he is a little more relaxed about talking about the birds and his systems. Will he miss the pigeons? Hard to say, but I do know that he is going to write a series of articles for the BHW in the coming weeks so after you have read this there will be more on the systems and winning ways at the distance by Jim Emerton.

How did you get started in the sport?

My father first introduced me to pigeons when I was a three-year-old living in Skegness. I am now 57 so I've been around pigeons for quite a few years. In those early days we had rollers, fantails, priests and various fancy breeds and crosses that we had many happy hours with. I have loved and been fascinated by pigeons since those early days. We settled at Holtby near York in 1976 and my original starting birds were the foundation of the 30-year-old Emerton Strain. The birds were mainly Descamp Van Hasten Stichelbauts with a direct cock from Emiel Denys and came from Louella lofts. An old fancier called Jack Ross introduced me to St. Lawrence pigeon club and off I started on a fantastic journey into the sport. I have a very perceptive eye for a bird and love all wildlife. When I was young I had a prophetic vision of forming a dynasty of champions around my number 1 pair it was a mystical experience and true.

With your pigeon work do you have a silent partner, i.e. wife, partner or friend, if so what part do they play?

My mother Dorothy helped with the birds until she was 91. Under my planning and guidance she carried out most of the tasks in the loft. She was very tough and tenacious and my achievements in the sport are largely due to her. She was a great friend to Eddie Newcombe and brought back many tips from Malta. Eddie was a believer in peanuts and through his success at the distance it helped to popularise them as a feed supplement for racing pigeons.

Do you consider there to be any advantage having a racing partnership?

Yes, you can share tasks and work off each other to achieve all the ambitions in the sport, and always remember that two united joint heads are better than one and the work can be shared. However, as in all partnerships of this kind there has to be an overall boss, and that was me.

Are there any points that you and your partner disagreed on?

Dorothy thought racing was cruel, but my vision for the future and my focus always settled matters. She also believed in discipline and control with birds and loft cleanliness, whereas I believe in an open loft and freedom for the birds at all times – freedom brings contentment and encourages endurance pigeons to home. In later years I was in a position to exchange well-bred pigeons with top fanciers, eg Chris Gordon, Jim Donaldson, T. Robinson etc.

Did each of you have an area within the partnership where responsibilities take control regarding a decision?

I made the overall decisions, my mother's help came out of love and dedication to her son. We had a formidable partnership, my mother being inspirational and very competitive.

Is there anything you have not won in the sport that you would have liked to achieve?

I am completely happy with my achievements in the sport from 71 to 879 miles with my strain. It was a long journey of progression from club to International racing

Did you hold any official position and if so did you take an active part? If not, what are your reasons?

I was a loner in this respect, but I used to be a Fed

delegate and a short-time President. My aim was to be a friend to all and avoid nasty disputes and negative politics.

What were your lofts made of, and how big were they?

I had a brick-built stock loft with aviary and small back garden loft made from wood and asbestos with plastic skylights. The loft was old when I brought it from Tadcaster some 30 years ago. It was seen as a joke as many thought it would fall down, but when it was finally disposed of many years later it took 15 man-hours to knock it down. Some of the modern-day lofts are nice and good, but pigeons don't worry about the décor. They require space, light, air and dryness. A tiled roof probably gives advantages in terms of ventilation. My loft did not have a tiled roof, and look at my overall performances.

Did you use any form of heating system in any of your lofts? Do you think it would be an advantage for the birds?

None. Heating is probably good for early term sprinters, but I had no room for sprinters unless they could fly over 700 miles. The control of temperature and humidity is very important for many of the professional sprint lofts to optimise the condition of those sprinters, and that is where they gain the edge.

How did you control the ventilation in your loft?
The loft in the latter stages was left open at the top, earlier ventilation controlled by aviary doors. My mother used to open the aviary doors for me during the day so that air was allowed to circulate through the loft structure itself. I never used grilles – far too modern. Pigeons like the comfort of deep litter. Grilles are good for hygiene but not cosy for the birds.

How did you go about bringing in a new family and what did you look for?
Only rarely have I done this. It must be an expert fancier with consistent National performances over 700 miles 2nd day usually eg with Trevor Robinson, a friend from his 9th open Pau 700 plus miles. The birds are ideally inbred to 'Key' pigeons with outstanding performances over 700mls such as Jim Donaldson from his Circus Boy/Dall Cock and Rennes Lass family.

When you bring in a new family do you think they need time to acclimatise, and if so how long?

Acclimatisation is a myth. Pigeon families are not genetically pure races, so they need no time to acclimatise. Only about 1% have been good enough for me at any time. That is to say pigeons that will perform well over 700 miles in top competition.

When looking for new pigeons do you look for a particular family, one for specialist races or club races or just by name?

I look for an excellent endurance family over 700 miles, not just a popular family name, eg Jim Donaldson, Neil Bush - they must be the UK's best. I am most impressed by the fancier, the honesty and integrity.

Which sex do you consider is the most important when it comes to breeding?

Both sexes can have equal influence on the progeny as they both carry the genes of the ancestral tree and these combine at fertilisation.

Does the size of the hen make any difference to the quality of youngsters that she breeds, in your experience?

Good breeding hens can be any size. It's the internal unseen factors that are paramount. I prefer small to medium hens always, as these birds are easier to condition.

When it came to breeding, did you line-breed or use a first cross, or just pair winners to winners?

I line-bred and inbred to inbred champions with the entire past top performances crammed into the pedigree. I liked to concentrate my breeding around key past and performance breeders such as Dark Destiny, Diabolos and Daughter of Darkness.

Do you think fanciers change for the sake of changing or do you think a loft can breed a winning team out and lose track of the winners?

Fanciers are carried away with buying pigeons and spending money, and they like a change. That is not the way to form a strain. It's easy to get carried away and spend large amounts of money on birds of dubious origin, and some fanciers like to keep up with the Joneses and lose track of where they are going.

What method did you use to select your breeders?
I chose silky-feathered balanced latebreds from my top performances. I kept the performance factors in the pedigree going. It is not possible to always select the best breeders, as the best characters are invisible. You need endurance ability; homing ability and speed are in part governed by genetic traits.

What materials did you use for nesting?
Plain dandy nests, warm and cosy. I have experimented with tobacco stalks, twigs and natural grasses but no matter what you use the pigeons have an instinct to build nests and they will gather what is at their disposal to achieve that goal.

How many stock birds did you keep, and did you breed off your race team? Also, how many pigeons do you think you need to breed off any individual stock pair each year to see if they are quality producers?
About 30 pairs of stock are needed to keep the strain alive. I bred off the race team as good birds can come from any pair. You need confidence and faith in your selection of stock, and remember that persistence and patience pay off in the long term.

What's the farthest distance you would train over?

I regarded 466 miles with the NFC as training for old birds, although I was always in the clock and many times with yearlings no training for young birds first time in a basket would be to race at between 90 and 140 miles. 200 miles first toss is too far for most young birds. Pigeons survive on their instincts. I have jumped birds 500 miles into Pau. I found that pigeons adapted to different circumstances with instincts controlling their behaviour.

Did you breed off the top widowhood cocks after the racing had finished? Did you breed late bred youngsters?

Late bred youngsters are fantastic for stock and these would be out of the performance races. I do not like late breds for racing. When racing late breds (hatched July onwards) they are generally lost.

How did you race your pigeons, and how many?

Natural all yearlings 466 miles NFC, all old birds 700 miles. I was feeding three good mixes together with peanuts, Hormoform, yeast, red band layers pellets in hoppers Thursday, Friday mix oil on corn Saturday, Sunday, Monday, Tuesday lemon juice on corn, Wednesday Bovril & probiotic Vydex in water. Thursday Aviform and in water. Before a big race, they would get a boost of Mycosan 'T' chlortetracycline in water. I would normally have 20-30 birds and all would be entered into races over 700 miles once they reached two years old.

Did you race your pigeons every week, or did you prefer to condition them for a specific race?

The yearlings that fly 466 miles NFC are the natural selections for the planned big races. As two-year-olds, everything has to be perfect. For the big ones the methods I used encouraged form for the marathon races.

In your view do you think that a loft needs different pigeons for different distances?

Out and out sprinters will only sprint. Some of my birds would win from inland to Pau. Some birds are only good for 700 miles. All pigeons are individuals and there are good and bad in most strains.

Is there any specific condition that your pigeons performed best at, or any particular time of the year?

Some hens are brilliant on small babies or eggs, they vary as individuals. Most of my good birds were hens because I flew the hens method. Of course pigeons are individuals, but you must always remember that good health and condition are paramount if you want to achieve the top results.

Did you use any floor dressing or did you clean the pigeons out daily?

Perches scraped out daily (mother was famous for that), a deep litter of shavings and easy bed, providing the excreta is dry. Religious cleaning is not necessary for pigeons.

Did you like to have plenty of room for the pigeons?

I tended to be overcrowded with the young birds in, but it didn't matter on open loft, my birds had free access to the great uncrowded skies.

Did you measure the amount that you give to each pigeon, or were they fed according to the individual?

I hopper-fed layers pellets and all the corn mix they would eat. The pigeons ate what they required, as we humans do.

Do you attach any importance to grits and minerals or can the pigeons get what they want they are out of the loft?

Grits and minerals were never given to the race loft as they found their own mixed grit minerals for stock. My races walked the fields for their requirements; remember that pellets are a complete feed.

Is there a way that your pigeons let you know when they were in form?

Buoyancy and lightness, change in personality, good performances in race build up. In the early days I won many pools by picking birds displaying vigour and positive changes in personality.

Do pigeons need any special treatment on their return from the race to help them relax? Is any such treatment needed for the short or long-distance races or the hard races compared to the easy races?

The multivitamin I used in the water was Chevita plus peanuts on trapping and rest. I used the Chevita multivit because it detoxifies and regenerates the muscle tissue.

For how many weeks do you think a pigeon can maintain its form on the widowhood system for both cocks and hens?

Up to 10 weeks may be possible; it depends on the individual pigeon and methods used.

A bird needs 2-3 weeks' complete rest, with no road training, before a big International race – its internal organs need to be lined with fat like a swallow emigrating to Africa. Birds can fly short channel races to say 400mls at 14-day intervals, especially when they are on the widowhood system.

What did you do when you were racing either widowhood or the roundabout when you had a bad race and lost a few of one sex?

Two cocks with one hen, two hens with one cock, fresh young hens in with the cocks or celibate. Pigeons are adaptable and soon go with fresh mates or can be flown without a mate at all, because their homing ability overcomes everything else.

Is a favourable loft location the single biggest factor in sprint racing?

Yes, and good racing methods. Many fanciers prefer the north-east corner with the prevailing south-westerly winds.

Did you treat pigeons differently with their preparation for the bigger races whether national, classic, specialist club or open?

Yes, they had more rest, carried more body weight and could be jumped 500 miles. All my birds had to go to national and/or International races.

Do you think a pigeon has the capability to race both short and long-distance races?

Pigeons are individuals, not just names. Some can race the entire programme of distance. Pigeons can race 800 plus miles on the second day.

Which is the more difficult, establishing a team of sprinters or distance pigeons, and why?

It is more difficult to establish 700 miles, as few will do it because it is relatively easy to build a team of sprinters based on the fact that more pigeons can fly shorter distances.

If you could pass on one piece of advice to fanciers old and young, what would it be?

Be ambitious, be your own person and dedicate all to your objectives make your own strain famous. Do not be intimidated by jealous, aggressive or negative individuals.

Did you race your young birds, if so how many races?

Latterly I did not race young birds; individuals can come from no training to sending them to the coast 220 miles. In the early years I was a young bird specialist.

They had plenty of training, then latterly no basket training and jumped into 140 miles for racing. I always liked my pigeons to have some experience of orientation home.

Do you consider that good pigeons will win in any position?
My Barcelona Dream raced in a north-east wind. It depends on the particular race. Usually birds win with a favoured wind, but sometimes birds win against the odds, and they may fly in the hours of darkness.

Some fanciers go out and purchase good quality winning pigeons but never appear to make the grade – why do you consider that this happens?
Some fanciers don't apply the correct management techniques – the fancier makes the bird.

Do you use the darkness system for the young birds, if so for how long? And do you think it affects them later in life?
Absolutely not – it may affect individuals in later life, although I have no evidence of this.

What criteria do you set down for the pigeons you winter with your thoughts on the following season?

Food, health, rest, plenty of exercise and good feeding. No rationing. I like birds to be plumb at the start of the season. Excess weight is soon taken off by driving cocks and rearing.

Are there any special treatments that you give your birds once the season has finished, and what do you recommend?

Control worms and canker give plenty of rich food for the moult. I separated my racers in January to rest them and prepare them for pairing in March. My stock were never separated.

If you could only give your pigeons one supplement what would it be?

Mycosan 'T' contains arsanillic acid and erythromycin. I believed it to be beneficial as I have faith in Chevita.

Which fancier has influenced you most in the way you fly your pigeons?

Emiel Denys with his cocks and hens out to Barcelona, also Geoff Kirkland's methods. Emiel was a specialist with hens and he won the Golden Wing at Barcelona twice.

Which champion pigeons over the years have left an impression on you?

The great 'Tee' of Emiel Denys and Lancashire Rose of J O Warren. Tee was regarded as the best Barcelona bird of his generation.

Do you consider that the eye has any importance?

I like to see a bright-coloured eye. With some fanciers eye-sign takes a religious or mystical proportion, but there is no basis in scientific fact for its predictive power.

What do you think can be done to take the sport forward?

Allow ETS for all. More national and international racing allow fanciers free excess to clubs. More freedoms for all, we need to be united for the common good of the big clubs.

What past mistakes have you learned from?

Incorrect training, too early mating of racers, listening

to poor advice. You need to gradually learn by your mistakes and try to perfect the system that suits you and your birds.

What qualities must a fancier have to be classed as a top fancier, and at what level must he/she have achieved results to be rightfully so-called a champion?

Intelligence, foresight, patience, ambition, dedication, success at national and international racing. A fancier needs an absolute and sustained long-term focus.

To encourage fanciers to either join or stay in the sport, what do you think about limiting prizes to two per race per loft?

Fanciers should jump into the deep end and sink or swim, learning to take knocks on the chin in pursuit of their set goals.

Is pigeon racing as a hobby going beyond the average working man? Is it becoming too technical and complicated, or can you keep everything simple and still win?

Everything is simple with pigeons and can be made so

at the marathon distance - natural birds still continue to win. Try to befriend a fancier who will help you to get your system right and on the road to success.

How do you consider the British sport is going compared to the continentals, and do they have any ideas that you think would benefit the sport in the UK?

Quite well. More international racing, as this is the best in Europe. The Belgium pooling systems are very good and their International organisation is the best.

What aspect of the sport interests you the most?

International racing, as this offers the biggest and best racing in Europe.

Is there anything that you do not like about the sport, something that you feel needs changing for the good of the sport?

Petty jealousy and club politics. Pigeon racing should be free to all in all areas. Too much emphasis on sprint racing.

If you went into another fancier's loft and were given the opportunity to leave with a pair of pigeons, how confident would you be that you had selected the best pair?

The factors that interest me are indetectable to hand or eye. Stamina, orientation and general potential are visible.

Any further comments?

I have travelled the world and applied everything I know to my birds. I have three entries in the Squills list of record performances. I think I have used my education and experience to good effect.

TRIBUTES TO JIM

From friends and associates

Chris Williams

Jim has made an outstanding contribution to the sport of pigeon racing, not only in terms of his well-documented race results and creation of a long-distance/marathon strain of pigeon, but as a writer, philosopher, personality, teacher, mentor and in my case, friend.

Since its inception in the 19th century the sport of pigeon racing has grown from a provincial pastime to a global phenomenon. I think it is fair to say that in recent years the profile of the British fancy has risen considerably, with UK lofts scoring several international wins, however the pinacol victory from the Catalonian capital, the prestigious Barcelona International has at the time I write these words has eluded the fanatical distance fanciers of Great Britain and the Irish republic. The sport of pigeon racing like life itself is a continual learning curve. It is also utopian in many ways because where else could you find construction workers, schoolteachers, miners, Arab princes, the Queen of England and the young, the old, the disabled all competing for a first prize in pigeon racing?

Here is where Jim Emerton the pigeon fancier, writer and yes, philosopher, comes to the fore. The creation of the Emerton strain of marathon racing pigeons has marked the culmination of years of study breeding and ultimately testing in what he refers to as 'race reality'. In laymen's terms, he has been there, done that and got the T-shirt.

I have been captivated by the magical mystery of pigeon racing in my own right from the age of twelve and have been writing articles on the sport since the age of 16. In that time I have amassed a great amount of respect for the knowledge, wisdom and wit that Jim freely shares in his books and articles. A short time ago I was asked to sit down and answer a few questions put to me by this colossus of the racing world. For a 29-year-old fancier keen to learn this was a dream come true, and being honest, it was a little nerve-racking. I answered the questions, then nervously pressed send on my email, all the time thinking 'what will such a respected and illustrious writer make of me, let alone my answers?'

That evening I went to bed not expecting to hear anything more, but how wrong I was. The next morning, in my inbox was a message from Jim thanking me for my reply, so now it was my turn to interview the man himself. What a joy it was to be able to go inside the mind of Jim Emerton, a man who many would say has set the benchmark when it comes to marathon racing in the United Kingdom. I set my mind to what I considered to be one of the greatest privileges in my time as a writer because during that process I learned so much from him, not only how to improve as fancier but as a pigeon racing journalist.

One of the great things about Jim's work is that

he continuously pushes the fancier and reader to think about things on a deeper level, similar to the great Greek philosopher Plato and his allegory of the Cave, which in brief describes how we can go through life accepting what we see, or we can go further and investigate what else is out there. In his written work Jim is continually trying to bring us fanciers to a deeper understanding of the racing pigeon.

Jim Emerton the man is highly intellectual, but for all this he keeps his feet firmly on the ground and is always willing to help and encourage fellow fanciers and writers. I know this from personal experience and because of this, there is no doubt in my mind that the work of Mr Emerton has brought the sport forward in a way that has not been seen since the great J W Logan. Thank you my friend!

Rod Carter I

Somewhere in York a door is slowly opened and an all-encompassing man with a rotund face and a genial smile beckons you into his humble abode. The smile broadens into a resounding grin which spreads across the manicured, bearded face of the genial master James Emerton. One can sense this is going to be another profound and enlightening afternoon with the man his intimate friends call Jim. What will be the first pearls of wisdom to fall from the mouth of this enlightened genius?

The air is electric with anticipation as he slowly and quietly utters the immortal words that will stay with me for ever, 'we are all just specks of dust within the entity that is the cosmos.' A sublime and enigmatic statement that comes from the very heart of the man. A man who can communicate with the lower echelons of human life as easily as he can with the academics and professors of this world.

Jim's wandering feet have carried him to many countries around the world, but now they are firmly planted on the carpeted floor of his residence. This main room is the hub of his small but far-reaching empire from which he communicates with a worldwide network of friends and acquaintances, all hanging on his every word.

When one meets Jim, it is all too easy to imagine an individual at peace with himself. But the smile and the quiet persona hide a darker side. Long ago in his distant past, his mind dragged the depths of hell, aided by substances no sane man should acquire a taste for. Floating on high, his mind was in an altered state of euphoric insanity waiting for the long spiralling journey to oblivion. Luckily he had friends to nurse him back to the mortal world, a world that he had left behind in a moment of mad experimentation.

Rod Carter II

What can one say, madman or genius? I think the jury is still out. l first met Jim working for York Parks Department. l can still see him now, hoe in hand, pipe in mouth and straw hat atop his head, standing in his park and surveying his domain like a majestic statue. If you were very lucky you could sometimes see him move, but this was usually only to relight his pipe.

Jim wasn't a very practically-minded man. Ask him to knock a nail in and he would probably pick up a screwdriver and ponder which end to use. No, Jim's tools are his razor-sharp mind and quick wit. Although he was a first-class gardener he was really more of an academic. His forte was as a union convener, sparring with management and wheeling and dealing with them for the benefit of the workers.

He was never more at home than at a union meeting wearing a big smile and a bright red T-shirt.

A teacher by profession who much preferred the outdoor life, he is slow of step and gentle of demeanour with pipe and beard as he ponders the vastness of the cosmos. One could imagine him in another life as a professor tutoring and giving lectures to lots of young, gorgeous female students (which would have definitely brought a smile to his now rather elderly features).

Does Jim have an ego, I hear you ask? Do horses have hooves, I reply. Jim's ego is the thing that propels him to keep up his hectic writing schedule. Without an ego I am sure he would vegetate into oblivion, becoming just another lost soul looking for direction. One of his profound sayings is that he perceives himself as just a speck of dust within the vastness of the universe. I'm sure this is what keeps his feet on the ground and keeps him so level-headed. So no, the doors in his house have not had to be widened, but a joiner is on standby.

Jim is not a practical thinker. His poetry stems from his experiences of life, mysticism, Far Eastern culture and the infiniteness of the universe. It is drawn from deep inside his psyche,in a trance, like a meditative moment of time.

To end this narrative of Jimbo, I will say he has a very humorous persona. Oddball maybe, one of a kind certainly, but with the wit and charm of somebody from the bygone age of romanticism.

Liam O'Comain

The Jim Emerton strain

Adapted from an article in Racing Pigeon Pictorial International, no 501

Jim Emerton's astute mind knew that in order to race marathon distances he needed the right goods, and it was a spark of genius when he decided to base his dreams of success on the historic Stichelbaut dynasty and the golden bloodlines of the 'Tee' etc. For from this base in due course came such outstanding thoroughbred athletes as 'Barcelona Dream', who was 13th Open British International Championship Club Barcelona at a record distance of 879 miles (an outstanding racer which succeeded against both east and north east winds); 'Dax My Girl', 31st National

Flying Club Dax 687 miles, longest flying bird out of 17,526 birds in Europe; 'Odd Ball', 3rd & 66th Pau (735 miles); 'Diamond Queen', 72nd Open NFC Pau; 'Dedication' and 'Sister Damien', 61st & 80th Open NFC Saintes 569 miles on the day; 'Mystical Queen', 10th Open SBNFC San Sebastian 737 miles, winning the Denney Shield for first bird over 700 miles into England; 'My Girl', 1st Section B, 4th Open Dax 687 miles; 'Dark Enchantment', 9th & 30th Section K Pau.

The loft has had the only bird in the clock station on the winning day at Sartilly YB 362 miles, Dax 687 miles and Barcelona 879 miles. Other good results have been obtained by others racing the Emertons in the BICC and the NFC. At least four NFC Section winners have been reported and other good performances from Marseille and Barcelona for others. In 2011, Trevor Robinson's two Barcelona birds at 853 miles were down from Jim's 'Dark Enchantment', inbred to Jim's No 1 pair.

Jim's birds were line and inbred for over 30 years. They were accommodated in a brick-built stock loft with an aviary and a small back garden loft made from wood and asbestos with plastic skylights. The ventilation was derived from an opening at the top and there were no floor grilles, not even in the nest boxes. Deep litter was used and it was estimated to be 15 years old on one occasion.

The racers were paired in the first week of March each year and without training the hens were lifted into racing between 90-110 miles and the cock birds between 110-140 miles. Jim has been known to lift birds 500 miles into races, seeking to discover their orientation ability. Jim placed a strong emphasis upon the pigeon's instincts at all times. Yearlings flew 466 miles and old birds 700 miles. Jim would normally have 20/30 birds and all would be entered into races over 700 miles once they reached two years old, always bearing in mind that pigeons are individuals and there are good and bad in all strains. When sending birds to Pau for example, Emerton liked his candidates to have had at least a 10 hour fly in a prior race. For International racing, 2-3 weeks' complete rest was required with no road training and the internal organs were lined with fat.

So there you are, Jim was a strain moulder who did not adhere to many theories apart from no more than four flights cast on racing. A man who reached for the stars and touched them. Jim is surely a unique individual who was an artist of the sport and one of the best Britain has produced in long distance and marathon racing.

Barry Phillips

One day back in September 1969, I headed north-east from Devon in my ancient white VW Beetle. My destination was the Royal Botanical Gardens, Kew, perhaps the most famous garden on earth. The following day, during our initial student assembly, two students immediately stood out from the 20 gathered at the Jodrell Laboratory: John 'Log' Whitehead from the world of arboriculture, forestry and trees and a smiling, cheeky-looking northern lad, James 'the brains' Emerton, from Yorkshire. It transpired that Jim was a true country boy with a massive passion for nature. Both these guys had very trendy Beatles-style haircuts. Given that my hair was also long, easily shoulder length, I immediately sense the beginnings of a bond between the three of us, but it soon became apparent that we had much more in common than our hair.

It soon became obvious that James was by far the

most intelligent of all the Kew students. After our initial three-month exam session, he was clearly on track for a distinction (over 75%) or Honours. 'Log' was a massively knowledgeable tree man, excelling in all the plant identification tests set for all students every two weeks. Academically I had to work much harder, but whenever the life cycles of ferns, fungi or seaweed came up I would lead the field because of my early studies at Exeter University under the distinguished Sir John Caldwell.

Jim was delighted for me when I did well academically, but like Log I came to the fore on practical subjects, vegetable gardens, plant identification and work projects, and when times got tough I always had Jim to turn to. The major difference, however, was that come the weekends, it was pens and books down, particularly for Jim, as it was time to party. Kew was perfectly placed on the Tube, just 30 minutes from Piccadilly and central London, so most weekends we were on our way into town to enjoy the mighty sixties/seventies sound of rock n' roll.

Our partnership began to flourish, Jim with his great sense of humour and undoubted charm with the ladies while initially I was the quiet, shy, reflective one, but very soon, having studied Jim closely, I was able to blossom myself in the charm offensive game.

I lived in a big house on Sandycombe Road, Kew, with another of Kew's notorious party animals, Alan Wilton, a second-year student from Cornwall. He was a big socialite on the music scene, president of the Kew Musical Group, Social Secretary for the Kew Mutual Improvement Society, indeed a man of many talents. One night, en route back home from a Pink Floyd gig in Camden, Alan and I were joined on the Tube by two stunning Swedish au pairs. By Richmond we were still chatting, and they asked if we could help them find a taxi to get them home to nearby Twickenham. I mentioned I had a car but there wasn't much petrol in it, and said they were welcome to stay at Sandycombe Road. They quickly agreed, and the rest is history as they say.

Margarita was one of the most beautiful girls I had ever set eyes on, blonde, slim and massively sensual. Early on the Sunday morning I drove down to Kew Green with her to Lena's famous café, and immediately spotted Jim. His Yorkshire tones echoed around the café: 'Eh up Barry, you've got a right beauty there,' he said. 'Yes Jim, but you didn't have to tell the whole of Kew Gardens,' I replied.

During our numerous moves around the many fascinating departments of Kew, we somehow managed to get involved in quite a few harmless pranks, generally involving the thousands of eerie cockroaches which inhabited the miles of heating pipes beneath the very famous giant glasshouses, especially the tropical Palm House. Jim was stationed there under the tutelage of Kew's most attractive supervisor, Ruth Stoor, a very pretty lass from Gloucester. His party piece was to collect 20 or so 'roaches' before Ruth appeared, tape a dozen or so to his clogs and march into her office at 8 am to the crispy, crunching sounds of the crushed roaches, the 'cockroach concerto' as we called it.

My cockroaches were trapped in my wellies, which I would leave in the heating pipes overnight. I would go quickly to the Insectivore House, open the section with the Venus fly traps and feed these creatures into their waiting jaws. This provided entertainment for the students and visitors looking for the 'man-eating plants' and I was able to photograph the sequence of events. I suspect no one other than me and Jim was any the wiser.

Life was generally good for us students of the finest

botanical gardens in the world. A few did drop out along the way, but the lads were certainly enjoying the London scene. We were reasonably well paid, very well housed and fed, and we were working in a great botanical environment, with some very eminent teachers and professors.

At weekends we were able to cut our teeth on some of the truly great rock bands of the early 70s such as the Who, the Rolling Stones, the Yardbirds, Black Sabbath and Robert Plant. In our second year we felt supremely superior to the 'fresher' intake assembled at our first Mutual Improvement Society meeting and wine and cheese. Jim and I were assessing potential new lads, and indeed lasses. But our main hunting ground was the big city, where our success rate was very high.

Jim had met a nice young lady called Susan, from East Sheen. One Sunday, June 18 1972, we all met up for lunch in the Orangery restaurant, aware that Susan's dad, a doctor, was flying to Sweden for a medical conference. Little did we know that tragedy was about to strike. Her father was on his way to a medical conference in Stockholm when news began to spread around Kew of a plane crash a mile or so south of Heathrow. At 5.30 pm Christine and I were in the Beetle en route to Devon when we saw plumes of black smoke coming from near Staines, where the ill-fated Hawker Siddeley Trident had crashed on take-off with no survivors.

We didn't see much of Jim for a couple of weeks after that as he was consoling his young lady friend – he was a very caring man. I seemed to see less and less of him, which may not be surprising in a 350-acre garden. That September I got married to the lovely Christine, but Jim had gone into his shell. He later confessed that he had days when he felt his brain was slowly grinding to a halt. He said he had found a place where he could climb Kew's 20ft wall and go home, or possibly to the pub for a quick half. On one occasion Christine had just turned into Kew Road when she saw someone jump off the Kew wall. He was limping, and yes, it was Jim. He asked her to join him for a cup of tea in Queen Anne's, a very posh restaurant on the Kew road. He confessed that he had been severely affected mentally by the tragic loss of Susan's father, and indeed he was very close to leaving the course and going home to Yorkshire. Christine implored him not to quit and invited him to come round to dinner with us. Later that evening Chris told me we had a special guest coming round to dinner, and as I walked down the stairs it was a wonderful surprise to see my great pal James at the front door with a bottle of Merlot. I had not seen him for almost a month, so a big hug was in order!

We immediately got back into the 'lad chat'. He told me later that he was presenting a talk on 'Racing pigeons of the world', but prior to that I had prepared a short item of interest, the rarest cycad of them all, Wood's cycad or *Encephalartos woodii*, a very rare endangered South African species which was down to single plants in the wild. We had one growing in the Palm House in Kew where I was working, and it was the only specimen known to be in cultivation and said to be over 200 years old. As the light dimmed for my slides I began talking about its pollination when I heard a squeaking sound from the audience – 'ee ee ee ee....' I immediately knew it was James, mimicking the sound of a rat and chuckling to himself in the front row. Regaining his composure, he raised his hand and said 'Barrington [the name he used for me], is it true that Encephalartos is pollinated in the wild by night flying bats, *Rufus rufus nocturnus africanus*?'

The predominantly student audience fell silent, eager to hear my reply.

'James, you are absolutely correct' I said. 'Indeed they are said to have a symbiotic relationship in that the Rufus excrement provides much needed manure in that harsh desert environment.'

Our 'Morecambe and Wise' comical double act became very popular, with topics being suggested by our fellow students. At one point we persuaded a beautiful young Indian lady, Jenny Law, to sit on a huge leaf of a giant of the Amazon, *Victoria amazonica*. Little did the audience know we had placed a stool to support our young model, scantily clad in a bikini. She was undoubtedly our most spectacular presenter of the year.

Notable additions to the normal crowd were Dr Chris Grey-Wilson and his herbarium colleague, Dr David Philcox, a real botanical character with a keen eye for the girls. Hence our Monday night crowd swelled from 30-40 in the early months to 50-80 by Christmas and compliments were coming from all parts of the gardens.

At the second-year presentation day James again got his academic prize with a massive 90% plus average in all the written exams. I picked up best practical and the vegetable prize. Some of the Kew hierarchy found Jim and me a little 'off the Kew wall', so for our third year we decided to conform just a little. As Year 3 students we had to set an excellent example and become more the leaders and less the eccentric entertainers, a role we soon grew into.

In the summer of 1972 I was granted a 'student exchange visit' to southern France, at the prestigious Jardin Exotique owned by M. Marnier la Pastolle on the French/Italian border, producers of Grand Marnier. I fear James did not participate, as he feared it might involve too much 'back-breaking activity'. Actually he was planning his next academic move, a two-year sojourn at the Worcester Training Academy. I was granted a one-year extension to prepare for a massive Himalayan plant-hunting expedition to North West Nepal, on the borders of Tibet. Almost 25 years flew by before two of Kew's most infamous lads were to reunite and rekindle a very special friendship,

Today in 2019, almost 50 years after our first Kew encounter, we happily remain in contact by phone or letter some 2-3 times a week. Time may have flown terrifyingly by, but our extravagant sense of humour has never waned or faltered. Often our quick-witted dialogue brings floods of happy tears to our eyes. We sing songs of yesteryear, often initiated by a quote or a memory of the past.

It has been wonderful to reminisce about this truly great, super-intelligent modern-day genius. It has been such a pleasure to be able to write with such pride about this honourable man and our early fun-filled years at Kew, great adventures and memories, a marvellous and inspiring experience for a humble guy from Devon to tag along for the past 50 years to a real superman of a human being, our Jim Emerton. Love ya mate!

Barry Phillips
Dip. Hort. Kew

Helen Mead, Features Writer

Jim has to be the most colourful creature to inhabit suburban York. On the outside he appears to fit the bill as a perfectly ordinary chap, shopping at Sainsbury's and popping to the paper shop every morning, but beneath that veneer is a man who lives on a different plane from everyone else. His personality has been shaped by a series of adventures in far-flung places such as Afghanistan and the Himalayas, as well as closer to home on the wilder reaches of the Norfolk coast. He has been in more scrapes than a child in a school playground and always comes out grinning.

Jim's intellect is in no doubt, and, for the common man (or woman), keeping up with his train of thought is impossible. A deep thinker, he always manages to see beyond the obvious and put a new, unexpected slant on a subject. He can throw you off guard in an instant with his perceptions and ready wit.

Jim never stops philosophizing, whether it is about buying a bag of potatoes or NASA'S latest mission to Mars. Or pigeons, about which he can talk for England.

Interview with Helen Mead, June 2019

'With a warm and helping wind, out of ancient and unknown urges, they attempt the epic flight of endurance to the Sahara. Young ones may linger until October in certain parts, and I recall little ones in the nests of the wash pillboxes in September. This migration is a living metaphor of man's ignorance of the subtleties and complexities of nature.'

These words, by poet and philosopher Jim Emerton, refer to the passage of the swallow, as the small bird makes its way on its intercontinental journey from Britain to North Africa. Our fascination with this annual ritual will never end, and despite countless studies through time, we will never really know how they, and other birds who make the gruelling trip, do it.

The feats of endurance undertaken by birds is a subject close to Jim's heart. He was once one of the world's top long-distance pigeon racers. Experiencing many successes in European races, he understands more than most how birds function. Yet even he does not pretend to really know all the answers. 'We are passengers on the planet, our transient and ephemeral existence bathed in ignorance,' he writes in his latest book, 'a singular swallow has the key to surely untold secrets.'

The Deep Thoughts of Jim Emerton is a collection of the former Bradford College student's more philosophical writings - his attempts, as he says, to 'verbalise the unknowable'. Jim, who studied trades unionism in Bradford, relays, in bite-sized chunks, his take on gargantuan subjects: 'Man, humanity and the meaning of life' is one chapter heading, 'Personality and the mind' another.

As perhaps is expected from an active member of Mensa – he has been a member since 1987 and regularly contributes to their literature – some of this is a little highbrow for most of us. Take the following: 'I accept the eastern influence of Taoism and Buddhism as tools of meditation. I see my mind as a microcosm led by the ego or pilot and like to access the deeper regions of its creative power... be careful what you tap into in conscious meditation, as it is a trip into the inner nature of the self, where you may encounter shadow and darkness before spiritual light.'

But beneath his intellectual ramblings, there is some sound sense and food for thought. He can also be funny, making light-hearted quips about life and characters. I use the word 'ramblings' as the book does jump about a little, with comments on subjects ranging from fashion and the guitar to life in the fast lane and money following in quick succession, as though he has quickly scribbled down thoughts as they race into his mind. I have met Jim, and, in this respect, the book reflects the man.

Sections from the book are reproduced with permission from Mensa Magazine. Indeed the paperback begins with an interview by the magazine's editor Brian Page, describing how, when travelling in Nepal, Jim began to develop his deep thought processes. He was on top of a mountain and experienced 'a complete loss of ego' and 'enhanced feeling of consciousness.'

Jim, who now lives in York, briefly explores 'the fusion of genius and madness', believing they are inextricably linked and combine to fuel creativity. He pens a poem about one of his heroes, Van Gogh, that begins 'each stroke of florid brilliance, an outpouring from the inferno. The need to purify, cleanse a troubled soul, And when the genius is projected, the retreat into the inner chamber of torment.'

A prolific author, Jim has written books on a range of subjects, from his love of nature to an in-depth look at his passion – the sport of pigeon racing. From his writing, few could fail to guess that as well as being an intellectual, Jim is an eccentric, and happy to admit to that. He certainly thinks outside the box.

The Chronicles of Jim Emerton

By Andrew Jenkinson (2019)

He's the personable bard of Heworth
With several books to his name
An outsize, monumental ego
Assuming posthumous fame.

His book sales are tops at Amazon
They are flying right off the shelf
His book about pigeons particularly
Sends royalties homing back to himself.

The 'Pigeon Man' book is illuminating
It's a relative bible to the bird
Quite a lifetime of experience
With enlightenment in every word.

He's the personable bard of Heworth
Writing ten thousand words before dawn
He writes to a very strict discipline
Cultivated since he was born.

The Deep Thoughts of Jim Emerton

Is a much more serious affair
He's the perfect philosopher's dream
A remarkable talent so rare.

With deep thoughts and mystical poems
Writing must seem just like fun
His output of words is tremendous
He's Shakespeare and Sartre rolled in one.

He's the personable bard of Heworth
His immense Mensa status gives gravitas
He writes for journals worldwide
Giving his profile a huge touch of class.

The countryman book is an intimate read
Of hardship and boy's own adventure story
Wildfowling out on the marshes
His prodigious birdcount brought glory.

It may be that Jim's *Life in Pieces*
Like the book with its title shows
He's packed in more lives than most
But his pot-smoking time still glows.

He's had a go as a metaphysical poet
When the creative urge suddenly strikes
But his credibility's out of the window
Like when he wears those blue £100 Nikes.

He once dabbled in horticulture
And learned all the plants' Latin names
Had a glorious spell working at Kew
But IQ was just one of his aims.

He's the personable bard of Heworth
Whose IQ's incredibly high
He can weigh people up in an instant
With the help of his perceptive third eye.

Jim lives in a world of academia
It gives him a right to hate work
His brain is so highly supercharged
But he can't tell butter from Stork.

The days of his youth are long gone
Of roaming under Lincolnshire skies
Naming the birds, trees and plants
Seeing them with countryman's eyes.

Today he walks round the village
Telling his audience tall tales
He might come across as all saccharine
But really he's tough as old nails.

Now the personable bard has reached seventy
An age when most people slow down
But Jim is still glued to his keyboard
And that leaves him wearing the crown.